BUSINESS PROCESS MANAGEMENT APPLIED TO BUSINESS EXCELLENCE & BENCHMARKING

Dr. Bernhard Hitpass
Dr. Jorge Román

Dr. Bernhard Hitpass
Depto. Informática
www.bpmcenter.cl
Universidad Técnica Federico Santa María
Santiago de Chile

Dr. Jorge Román Gárate
Business Excellence Chile Ltda.
www.businessexcellence.cl
Santiago de Chile

All brands and names mentioned in this book are registered trademarks or marks of their organizations. Any omission or misuse should not be interpreted as an attempt to trespass other properties. The published recognizes and respects all marks used by organizations to distinguish their product rights.

No part of this book may be reproduced or used in any form, graphic, electronic, photocopy, without express written permission of the publisher, except for brief quotation references in articles, scientific journals, and conferences.

This book aims to the use of Business Process Management (BPM) with Business Excellence and using Benchmarking for Best Practices for public and private sector.

All rights reserved
Editorial: BHH Ltda. - Santiago de Chile
Copyright © BHH Ltda.
First Edition: June 2020

ISBN: 9798647651945

PREFACE

An organization needs to control their business processes in real-time, otherwise:

- We do not know, if we are delivering the committed value proposition
- We do not know, what is the state of the process execution, without an analysis activity
- We can't answer a customer claim immediately
- What we can't measure, we can't improve it
- You can lose control in order to determine if their goals are being met

The discipline that allowed to define and implement the business process logic for execution in real time, is called Business Process Management (BPM), here comes BPM in play, as a recommendation to implement and execute a customized Business Excellence Framework.

Business excellence models are frameworks (BEF) that, when applied within an organization, can help to focus thought and action in a more systematic and structured way that should lead to increased performance. Facing an increasingly turbulent and chaotic environment, more and more companies have implemented business excellence strategies and made quality a key element of their business philosophy as quality leads to improved business performance. The value of the Business Excellence Framework is intentionally non-prescriptive. It does not tell leaders how to manage their organizations.

The book explores an effective strategy for Business Process Management applied to Business Excellence and Benchmarking within any type of organization: big or small, new or old, private or public. It is written to guide leaders of any profession to not only improve their knowledge in processes but also in Business Excellence and Benchmarking. It is a holistic approach to developing a sustainable, successful business no matter its starting point. Unlike many existing books to use Business Process Management (BPM), this book offers a unique value because of its user-friendly, linked the best of BPM with BEF and Benchmarking, straightforward, fun-to-read approach.

Current and future managers and decision makers gain the knowledge and skills they need to achieve organizational excellence. With a focus on continually developing the quality of people, processes, products, and the work environment, it covers all pertinent quality-related topics, including: an overview of quality, quality and global competitiveness, strategic alliances, establishing a culture of quality, customer satisfaction and quality, employee empowerment, business process management, leadership and change management, team building and teamwork, education and training for quality, overcoming internal politics and conflict, quality tools, problem solving and decision making, quality function deployment, statistical process control, continuos improvement methods such as PDCA, TQM, lean management, benchmarking, six sigma and benchmarking, just-in-time/lean manufacturing, and implementing quality.

The book will cover the following:

1. Business Process Management (BPM)
2. Industry 4.0: The New Age of the Smart Industry
3. Continuous Improvement Tools & Techniques
4. Business Excellence Frameworks
5. Adoption of BPM and Business Excellence Framework
6. Benchmarking

The purpose of this book is to demystify the elusive process applied Business Process Management to BEF and Benchmarking in any type of organization and to creating quality culture through simple and easy-to-follow instructions. Big or small, public or private, every kind of organization has the potential to operate with a quality culture.

The authors of Business Process Management applied to Business Excellence and Benchmarking are both a university professor and an experienced international consultant. In addition to their academic background, the authors have years of consultancy expertise, bringing a great deal of practical advice to their approach.

Reader notes: Several sections described in the BPM part of the book are summaries and updates to Prof. Hitpass' academic books and papers [1], [2], [3], [4], [5]

This book, quite literally, would not exist without the Pandemic 2020. During the lock-down we had the discipline, perseverance, time and determination to finished and published our book.

Acknowledgments

We would like to express our deep gratitude to our colleagues and organizations around the world that inspire and help us to finish this project.

Special thanks to Dr. Robin Mann from Massey from Centre for Organizational Excellence Research (Massey University in New Zealand); Professor Mohamed Zairi, CEO of Excellence Tetralogy in UAE; Dr. Yasir Alnaqbi Leadership and Government Capabilities at Prime Minister Office-UAE; Antonio Bonani, Mining Resources Manager at Codelco-Chile; Professor Tariq Aldowaisan CEO of Global Lead Consultants, Kuwait; Cyndi Laurin, Ph.D Founder of the Guide to Greatness-USA; Benito Flores, Dean of Engineering School at UDEM-Mexico; Dr. Saleh Alhamrani, Deputy Director of Excellence & Pioneering Dept. at Dubai Police-UAE; Dr. Jose Luis Gallizo University of Lleida-Spain; Alejandro Lifschitz Ferrous Raw Materials Manager at Aceros AZA-Chile; José Antonio Martinez CEO and Andres Araya CIO Santiago Stock Exchange, Fernando Barraza Director of SII Chile; Dr. Hernán Astudillo, Universidad Técnica Federico Santa María, Chile.

Our special thanks to Dubai Police, Centre for Organizational Excellence Research (Massey University in New Zealand), Dubai Government Excellence Program, BPM Center Chile and Business Excellence Chile.

Thanks to partner and good friend Dr. Bernhard Hitpass for this journey.

TABLE OF CONTENTS

1 **Business Process Management (BPM)** 8
    1.1   *Introduction to BPM* 8
    1.2   *The Organization and the Structure of BPM* 10
    1.3   *BPM Governance* 10
    1.4   *BPM Operational* 11
    1.5   *Process Architecture* 13
    1.6   *Tools for BPM* 20
    1.7   *Process Automation* 24
    1.8   *Process Controlling* 26
    1.9   *BPM Challenges and Benefits* 30

2 **Industry 4.0: the new Age of the Smart Industry** 31
    2.1   *Industry 4.0 and IoT* 31
    2.2   *Characteristics of processes in Industry 4.0* 32
    2.3   *Relationship exists between Industry 4.0 and BPM* 34
    2.4   *Define the digital transformation strategy for your organization* 35
    2.5   *Examples of Best Practices in Digital Transformation* 37
    2.6   *Industry 4.0 Challenges for BPM and e-Commerce* 40

3 **Continuos Improvement Tools and Techniques** 41
    3.1   *PDCA: The Deming Cycle* 42
    3.2   *Six Sigma* 43
    3.3   *KAIZEN* 46
    3.4   *Lean Management* 50

4 **Business Excellence Frameworks (BEF)** 54
    4.1   *The Malcolm Baldrige Framework* 55
    4.2   *The EFQM Model* 64

	4.3	Singapore Business Excellence Framework	74
	4.4	Dubai Business Excellence Framework-4G	76
5		**Adoption of a BPM Business Excellence Framework**	**79**
	5.1	Business Excellence Framework and their integration with BPM	79
	5.2	Example of Adoption of a BPM integrated BEF	80
	5.3	BPM Business Agility with DevOps	82
6		**Benchmarking**	**86**
	6.1	Introduction	86
	6.2	Benchmarking for Best Practices	90
	6.3	Dubai: We Learn Initiative	95
	6.4	Dubai Police Case Study: Call of Duty (TRADE Methodology)	96
	6.5	Business Process Management integrated with Benchmarking	100
	6.6	Summary	101
7		**Appendix**	**103**
	7.1	Acknowledgement to the Reader	103
	7.2	Glossary	104
	7.3	List of Figures	105
	7.4	About the Authors	107
8		**References**	**109**

1 BUSINESS PROCESS MANAGEMENT (BPM)

1.1 Introduction to BPM

Globalization is demanding more requirements, to both private companies, and public organizations, in their ability to react to changes required by the market. These include changes in the type of demand or change in regulations.

The ability of organizations to adapt their offers of goods and services are a basic part of the new concept of customer value. The products themselves are not adequately attractive, because there is usually an oversupply of them, and the differentiating element is primarily the services around these products. These challenges include the compliance of internal, external, and international regulations, focused on quality control (traceability), fraud prevention, and care of the environment. Introducing processes in organizations to enable them to enter a virtuous cycle of continuous improvement to meet these requirements through time, which are the current challenges that organizations depend on [2].

Many people become confused with what really BPM is, which is not surprising considering that the BPM community has failed to agree on a common definition. Currently there are many definitions of BPM. Although they all have something in common, there are also differences, especially in the scope. Some authors and experts, mainly in Europe, explicitly restrict the BPM management discipline without including IT support. Other authors, define BPM as the process to the automation and operation of processes implicitly with IT. Can we conclude then that there is no common understanding on BPM?

The concept of BPM is even wider than both visions recently described, but common understanding can be achieved through the aims followed with BPM, which generally share all schools. Differences among schools are usually found in the concept on how to deal with the process to achieve these aims; each concept starts with a definition, which is the reason that some definitions differ from others. Goals description is clear and well defined:

- Achieve or improve "business agility" in an organization. The concept of business agility is the ability of an organization to become adapted to the changing environment through changes in its own integrated processes.

- Achieve greater "effectiveness". The concept of effectiveness is the ability of an organization to achieve, to a large or a lesser extent, the strategic or business goals.

- Improve "efficiency" levels. Efficiency is the relationship between the results accomplished, and resources used, i.e., productivity of a result. The term efficiency relates to all productivity indicators of quality, costs and time.

Today, for an organization it is not enough to be only efficient, as it could have been formerly; if this organization can not adapt itself to the frequent changes driven by globalization, it is not effective. It does not fulfill the targets demanded by the markets, in time and quality. Most of all, business agility has become more important in our times of globalization. The company that can adapt itself more rapidly to constant changes in the market, more and more frequent every day, will take greater competitive advantages over those that can not adapt themselves to the pace required by the globalization.

The crucial question is then: What tools are using companies to achieve greater agility, efficiency, and effectiveness? The answer is more control and efficiency in the ability to change their business processes, because value for customers is created through processes. How? Since early 90's, it came to life in industrialized countries integrating different corporate management disciplines directly with the processes operation. A Smith and Fingar publication in 2002, entitled BPM Third Wave [6], came up for the first time with the acronym BPM. Academics, professionals, and IT vendors quickly grasp the importance and interest in BPM. The trend keeps growing every day, which favored a strong investment in the development of techniques, methodologies, and solutions for BPM.

BPM is an integrative discipline that includes techniques and disciplines, covering layers of strategy, business, and technology, which are understood as an integrated whole in management through processes.

BPM encompasses all those analyses and process-oriented management practices that help to improve the efficiency and effectiveness of services producing value. People's development is a key factor to identify themselves with the assigned tasks; also, to be involved in further actions and in the accomplishment of the enterprise goals. Implementing BPM becomes, simultaneously, an enterprise strategy to achieve higher levels of organizational excellence. It is highly correlated with "Business Excellence Models".

1.2 The Organization and the Structure of BPM

BPM as a process-oriented management discipline covers two major areas of business management:

- BPM Governance and,
- BPM Operational

The BPM Governance concept is a process oriented corporate management framework, while the BPM Operational concept includes the entire management cycle for each process, or business line separately. Each process may be at a different maturity level concerning its BPM implementation; on the other hand, BPM Governance is only a corporate management framework for all the areas of the organization. These two basic concepts are hereunder described and analyzed for a better understanding of BPM.

1.3 BPM Governance

We will define BPM Governance, also called corporate governance, as a process oriented corporate management, but integrated with all organization's layers, the phases of the management cycle, change management, organizational structure and all the alignment instruments in, and between corporate structures. BPM Governance includes the entire corporate management cycle alignment, from planning and strategic management, definition of business plans, budget cycle, definition of profiles and positions, management in operations, and technology support, to the alignment with the corporate project portfolio. In literature there are several definitions of BPM Governance most of them very wide, but they all agree that this is a concept defined for an organization, on how should be "Process Management" applied, integrating the existing tools and disciplines around business processes.

Harmon [7] discriminates earlier between "governance" and "management", explaining that "governance" is the organization of the "management". Summarizing, to his understanding, when it comes to governance, we mean a management specific framework, while "management" is a human activity.

To Jeston and Nelis [8], in a BPM Governance model are key elements of the definition of roles and responsibilities, the process of alignment with the corporate strategy, the process-oriented management, and finally the standardization of management processes.

Kirchmer [9] defines "Business Process Governance as a set of guidelines focused on organizing all BPM activities and initiatives of an organization to manage all of its business processes. The resulting governance framework provides the frame of reference to guide organizational units of an enterprise and ensure responsibility and accountability for adhering to the BPM approach. In its simplest terms, BPG can be considered the "definition" layer of BPM and contributes to the definition and allocation of power and authority in the enterprise by specifying the governance framework".

1.4 BPM Operational

In the author's understanding the Operational BPM involves BPM process-based cycle management (see figure 1), and not the mechanisms of alignment with other layers of the organizations, which are the BPM Governance model domain. The cycle shown in this book is intended to be applied to each process separately or independently. Each process can be in a different state of the cycle. The cycle starts from two possible constellations:

- A current process that must be surveyed and documented and/or re-designed
- A new process must be introduced, inexistent in the organization

In the Surveying Process phase, the first step is to collect information on how the workflow is organized. This is carried out with the help of moderation techniques, workshops, interviews, gathering of documentation, etc. To this effect, the following should be considered in the surveying process:

- Clear delineation of prior or subsequent processes
- Describe the services it produces for the clients and the priority they have from the point of view of business objectives
- Represent both, the workflow and the roles involved in each of the steps, resources used and the information systems that support it

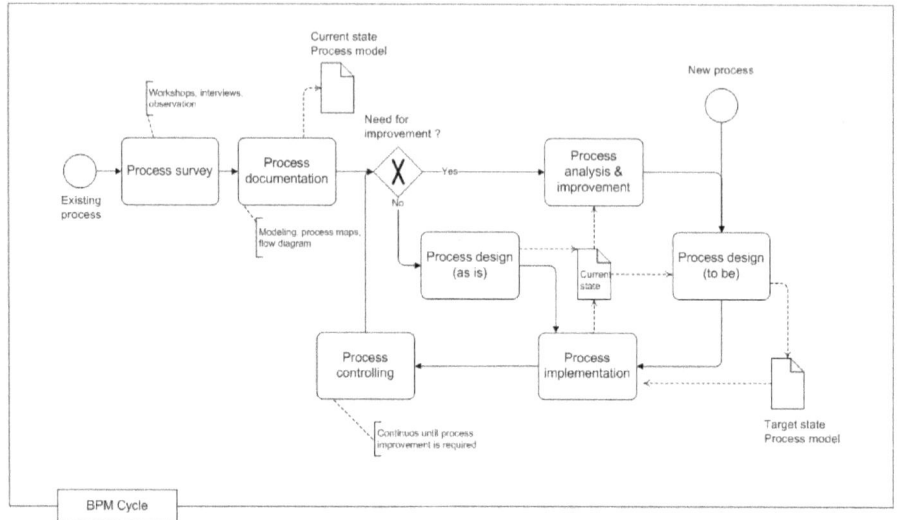

Figure 1: BPM Process-based cycle

At the "Process Documentation" stage, the knowledge acquired in the surveying phase is recorded in a process model that reflects the current situation. The resulting documentation includes the flow charts, description sheets, business policies, and procedures used to perform the job. Weaknesses identified at the stage of "improvement analysis" or deviations of the "Process Controlling", are usually the starting point for a process redesign. The different variants or scenarios can be eventually evaluated using simulators. This also applies if a new process is being designed. In both cases, the result or deliverable is a desired process framework (To be).

The "Implementation Process" involves both, technical implementation and organizational adjustments required. The change management and communication strategy are key elements to consider for the project success. The technical model can be implemented by a BPM Suite (BPMS) or through a software classical programming. The result of the process technical implementation is the current situation (As is) automated and recorded, equivalent to the desired process model. The phases from the "Surveying Process" to the "Process Implementation" are generally managed through the organization of a project, while the "Process Controlling" is conceived as a continuous process and is part of all operations. The most important activities of "Process Controlling" are the constant operation control and its relevant evaluation of indicators. According to the BPM school, if specific problems are detected they should be immediately corrected. If resources are available practical problems can be solved without having to formulate a project, but if the causes are not clear or perhaps complex, it is necessary to plan and implement an improvement and redesign project. The decision on whether to develop a new project or set up a task force in operations, should be taken by the person responsible for the process with the mutual consent of the participants.

With this brief explanation on how the BPM cycle works, the reader will realize the importance of BPM process models and along with it, how important a modeling and execution standard as BPMN (Business Process Model and Notation) may become. The reader may also confirm that the "process modeling" activity is not a BPM cycle stage, but rather a transversal activity, because it is applied in almost all phases of the cycle, especially in the phases of "Process documentation", "As is design", and "To be design". Unfortunately, we always meet people who confuse "the Process documentation phase" with the process modeling and include it as a phase in the cycle; that is a mistake. The BPM cycle shows in its main phases how the virtuous cycle of continuous process improvement of processes works. To apply this, it is necessary:

- Assign responsibilities to the processes and to each of its steps
- Use analysis and management methods in it
- Having the support of IT appropriate solutions

The task of management by processes (BPM-Governance) is to accomplish a smooth coordination between these three components. Management by processes is above any modeling project and therefore has the mission of supporting the "Operational Process Management" for the fulfillment of the strategic objectives.

1.5 Process Architecture

Process architecture abstractly represents at a very high-level process areas that are required to run a business. According to the school that the readers consult, they will find different types of configurations and different terminology. Currently, there is no standard in the BPM Domain that defines the terms, elements and how to represent a process architecture graphically.

The process architecture, which we present in this work and in accordance with the proposal from Hitpass [2], describes the value configuration model for a business model and all process models that depend on configuration at various levels of decomposition, up to arrive at the processes that describe the business logic in operations (flow diagrams).

The Hitpass proposal for a process architecture consists of 3 layers and 5 levels. The first layer represents the management processes; the second, the business or operations layer; and the third, the layer of support processes. The processes of the management layer and those of the support areas are generally quite standardized globally and are quite independent of the industry in which they operate. In the business or operations layer there are large differences in value configurations depending on the item.

Levels	Management Layer	Business&Operation Layer	Support Layer	Notation
Level 1	Process maps	Configuration Value	Process maps	Value Added Chain (VAC)
Level 2	Process area	Process area	Process area	Map
Level 3	Process life cycle	Process life cycle	Process life cycle	VAC
Level 4	Management processes	Business processes	Support processes	VAC & BPMN
Level 5	Business logic	Business logic	Business logic	BPMN

Figure 2 Structuring levels of the process architecture

Figure 2 shows the 5 levels of decomposition for each of the organizational layers. From a conceptual point of view, the business layer differs from the other two at the first level, where the type of value configuration required in the process architecture for a specific business model is shown. As the other two layers do not require special treatment, we only focus on defining the process architecture for the business layer.

According to the concept of value, the process architecture represents the value creation phase, that is, the "how" products and services are generated from the value proposition of a specific business model.

The concept of value configuration was developed by Stabell [10] as an extension of the value chain concept described by Porter, because the value chain is better suited to explain the situation of manufacturing, retail or logistics companies, but not necessarily for other sectors.

Service companies, which carry out their activities in a wide spectrum, ranging from health services, and schools to financial intermediaries, would not see their value dynamics reflected using this technique. Below we will describe a proposal of three types of value configurations according to Stabell [10] to represent the first level of a process architecture.

1.5.1 The value chain

Value chain models are proposed as long linked and sequential technologies. In a manufacturing company, value is created through the transformation of inputs to products. Figure 3 shows the generic value chain.

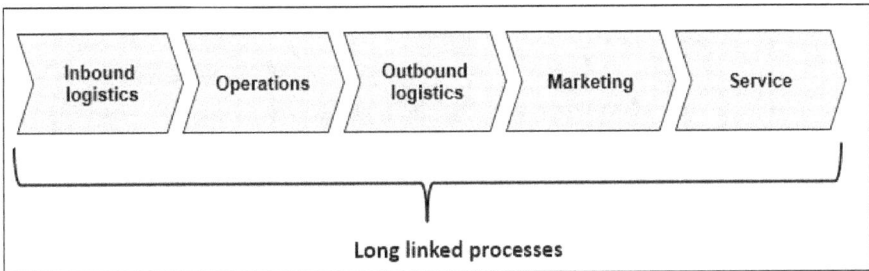

Figure 3 Representation of value chain type configuration

The business processes of the value chain type configuration are characterized by having a long link that goes from inbound logistics processes to post-sale customer services. The items of manufacturing, retail and logistics companies follow this type of value configuration.

1.5.2 The value shop

The name "shop" alludes to the fact that a business model is configured in a cycle, aimed at solving customer problems. Problems can be defined as the differences between an existing and a desired state, so the solution of problems (and therefore the creation of value) in (work) shops is to achieve that desired state. For example, in the area of health, the change is to cure the patient of an illness; In the case of architecture, the change is to build a building on a site. The intensive technology is then directed to obtain the desired changes in a specific object of customer interest. Professional services, health and education could, according to the business model approach, belong to this type of value configuration.

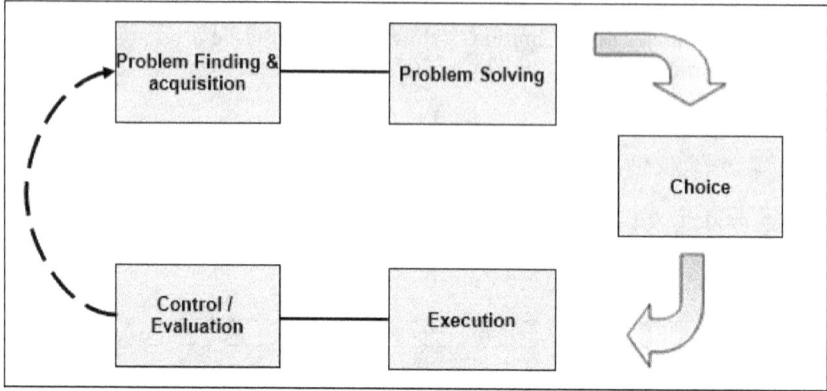

Figure 4 Representation of value shop type configuration

Figure 4 shows the cyclical nature of the links, which is captured by the circular distribution of the primary processes, where the post-execution evaluation can be the search for problems from another cycle of problem solving.

1.5.3 *The value network*

Finally, there is a type of configuration, where the value proposition starts with a business object (operating infrastructure), and around this object more and more services are offered. For example, in a transport company, the business object is the ship, the plane, the bus, etc., and each business has its main service, in this case, the transport of something. Then, in addition to transportation, additional services are generally offered that add value. For example: duty free, VIP lounge and internet services in commercial airlines.

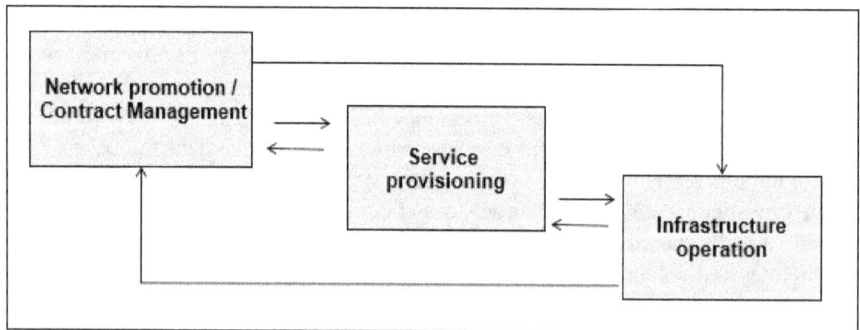

Figure 5 Representation of value network type configuration

Figure 5 shows the generic value network diagram. In the value network, operational infrastructure is the main business object.

For example, a hotel could not offer accommodation if it does not have rooms to accommodate its customers. A hotel infrastructure can offer, in addition to accommodation, event rooms, restaurants, a gym and Mini-Buses for transportation. Around this infrastructure it can offer autonomous or combined services, for example, events with accommodation, food and transportation. Figure 6 shows the value configuration of the network type, as the first level of the process architecture, for a hotel business.

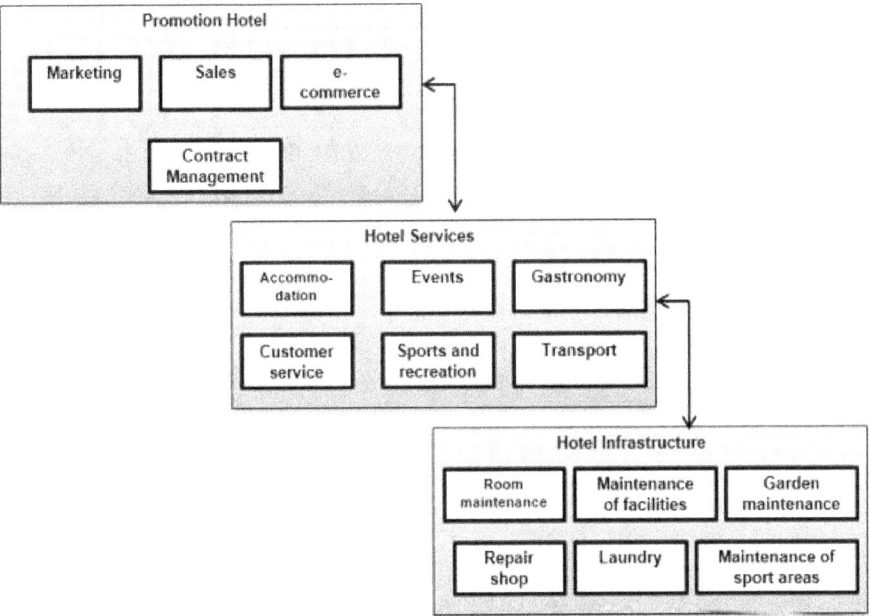

Figure 6 Value network of a hotel

1.5.4 *From process map to business processes*

In the process architecture proposed by Hitpass, it recommends creating a process map for each link in the value configuration. A process map is defined as an enumeration of process areas. For example, "Accommodation" and "Events" are process areas. These process areas generally correspond to organizational units. Process areas contain, in turn, processes that need to be run at the configuration map

17

to create the products and services of the business model. Each process area has a life cycle. They are processes that go from the creation of a product or service to its evaluation, post-sale or closure.

A process area has a life cycle, because before offering services to customers, business processes must be planned, modeled, developed and released. They are then managed in operations and, the final part of the life cycle, corresponds to the performance evaluation of the executed processes.

Figure 7 shows the value cycle of the events process area of a hotel business. It can be clearly recognized that the business process encompasses "from sales to events."

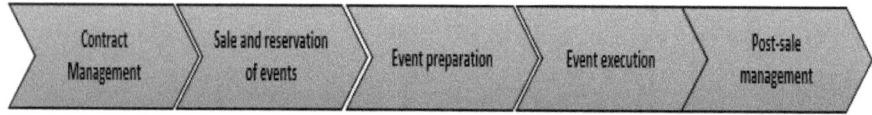

Figure 7 Life cycle process area events

These are the business processes that are in contact with the client. However, the "contract management" processes correspond to activities that prepare the business to be able to offer it.

Each of these processes in the life cycle of a process area contains business logic that can be technically automated as a workflow in information systems.

Figure 8 shows the business process Event Management in the BPMN notation the flow diagram with descriptive level "from sales and reservation of events - to event execution (realization and billing).

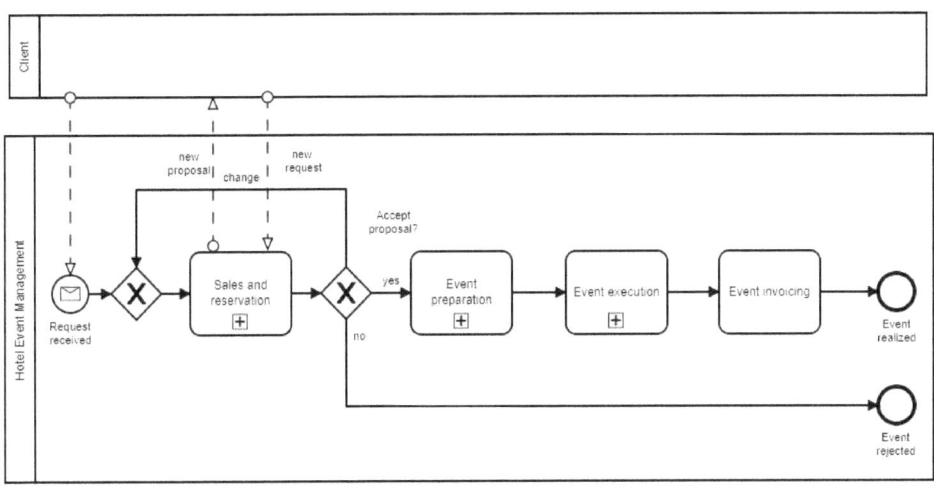

Figure 8 Business Process Event Management

As an example, we will now describe the business logic in BPMN of the subprocess "sales and reservation" thread in detail at the operational level (see Figure 8).

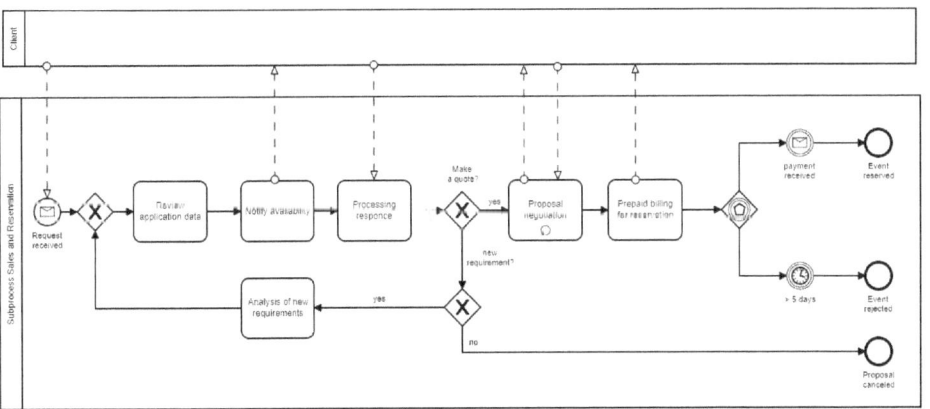

Figure 9 Subprocess sales and reservation of an event (BPMN detail logic)

The subprocess is triggered by the receipt of a request for a quote by a client. The application data is reviewed, and the availability of rooms, equipment and personnel is verified. The possible dates of completion are then communicated to the client (activity: notify availability). The following activity processes the client's response, and in the case of no agreement on the available dates, it returns to the initial flow and other alternatives are sought.

If the client confirms an offered date, the official quote is prepared. It is a synchronous activity, which is repeated so many times until an agreement is reached. The last activity in this process is to bill a prepaid amount. If the payment is received, the end event of this subprocess triggers the start event of the following process: "Event preparation".

The business logic in this example spans the entire workflow at the user activity level. This process described at the operational level in BPMN can be automated, if the specification of the control flow does not violate the syntactic rules of the notation. For each activity, Key Performance Indicators (KPI's) can be defined to measure the performance in real time of the process.

1.6 Tools for BPM

Many companies request expert advice support to carry out a BPM tool selection process. Some other companies are already planning to buy a BPMS (BPM System) and want to support their decision asking to a BPM Center about the image, seriousness, and prestige that the software provider might have. Many other institutions buy full BPM suites without even having the aim of process management, often driven by market trends and bold pre-sales presentations from leading market players. In both cases, we must first ask: A BPM tool to do what? The answers are as varied as application areas the discipline of process management can have (BPM). Here are some of them:

- Well, first we have to map and design our business processes!

- We want to start with a prototype to gain experience!

- We need to integrate us in real-time into the Finance Agency!

- Competitors take less than 5 days to approve a mortgage application!

The crucial question is then, is it possible to meet all these requirements by acquiring only one BPM suite? While the term suite indicates that it is an integrated platform containing several components, it is also true that although it is a suite, they are still specialized environments and if so, they are not universal.

If the idea is to design or modeling a process, we are speaking about an analysis process. And if we are considering BPM Governance, we have a management methodology. If we think of producing a prototype, we are speaking about testing an implementation environment or process automation. And if we think of shortening the life cycle of a process, we have optimization and control techniques through indicators.

All these objectives make reference to different BPM application areas. Each application area is a BPM specialty and relies on different concepts. Then, it will be hardly difficult to find a universal tool covering all these areas; on the contrary, it would be an aberration trying to build a BPM universal suite.

As a comparison, let's analyze a practical example: A Ferrari or a Porsche are not suitable for traveling over rough terrain like a jeep, and it is unthinkable that a Jeep or a Land Rover will win a Formula 1 race. This also applies in BPM, a BPMS suite will not be useful to represent a strategic map and align it with a company's process. Nor is it to describe business policies and rules, independent of the processes that they use. In the first case we are talking about a BPA (Business Process Analysis) suite, and in the second case, about Rule Engines called BRMS (Business Rules Management Systems). As the reader has noticed, the well-known BPMS has been just one component of all the BPM application areas, which involve the technical implementation and process automation.

In general, the BPM tool market can be segmented as follows:

- Tools that support the analysis processes and Corporate Governance (Governance BPM) called BPA platforms (Business Process Analysis) or EA (Enterprise Architecture Tools) as well.
- Tools that support the technical implementation or process automation called BPMS.
- Tools that support the business rules administration and execution, independently of the systems they use, called Rules Engines or BRMS (Business Rules Management Systems).
- Tools that together with processes enable to implement the management control indicators in real time, called BAM (Business Activity Monitoring).
- Tools that enable the services orchestration between BPMS and any type of system, mainly those from back office, called SOA Suite.
- Tools to analyze historical data from processes implemented to detect deviations from the desired behavior or discover new patterns. These analytical environments are called Process Mining Tools.

BPM experts know that depending on the requirements or complexity of an organization, it might be necessary an even finer decomposition, for example, to separate a BPMS presentation layer or decompose SOA-Suite in several specialized environments (ESB, SOA Repository, etc.) All these tools can be positioned at three levels or layers of a modern Entrepreneurial Architecture framework, as shown in Figure 10

The business layer covers the entire cycle of planning, analysis, management, and controlling of the strategy and business model. These tools support all the features for documenting the plan, analyze, model and keep the change control of requirements under integrated models in a common database, are called EA (Enterprise Architecture) or BPA (Business Process Analysis) Tools.

The reader should not confuse BPA Tools with tools that were designed for modeling and implementing processes, such as the widespread Bizagi license free tool. Also, it is important not to confuse diagramming tools like MS Visio with BPA tools. With MS Visio, the analyst is free to diagram whatever he might imagine, and diagrams have a good print quality, but they don't have any other functionality, as those needed for BPM Governance, like versions, attributes, and user management, impact analysis, animation, and simulation, etc.

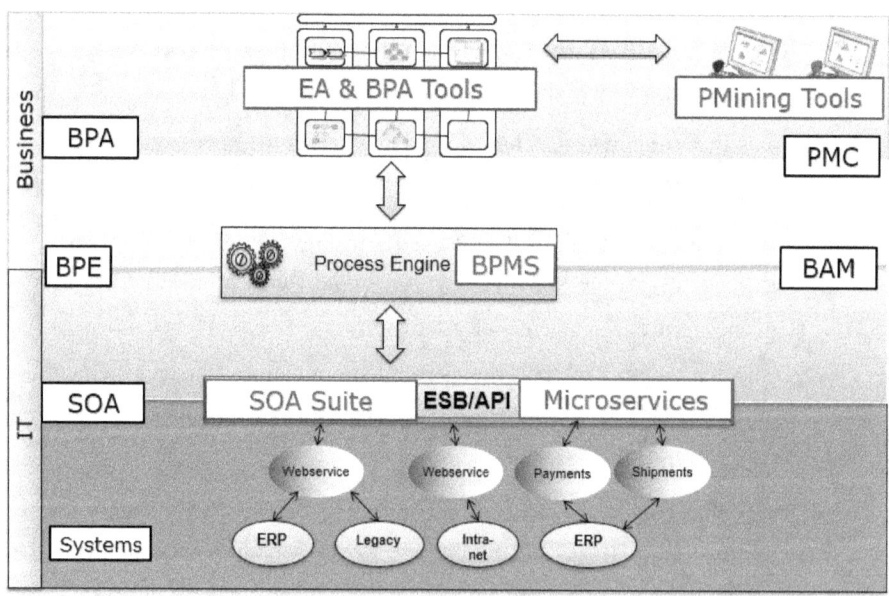

Figure 10: Platforms and tools for BPM

What tools can be classified as true BPA Tools? In the market we can find tools such as ARIS, IBM-BPM, Archimate tools, Troux, among others.

The second and third layer called BPE (Business Process Execution) covers both, process technical implementation and services orchestration, and integration in the SOA layer (Service Oriented Architecture) or with the new trend Microservice orchestration with the back-office applications.

A "microservices architecture" is a concept to developing a software application as a series of small services, each running autonomously and communicating with each other. As benefits with respect to the webservice architecture (more monolithic) we have to:

- A microservice can be deployed independently: a change in the module will not affect the others, we will only have to upload that module.
- It is easy to understand, since the business logic is well separated.
- Facilitates the management of multifunctional and autonomous teams.
- It is easier to scale at the software level, since instead of replicating the entire application and managing it with balancers, the microservices with the most load will be replicated

In this layer we find the well-known BPMS, as IBM BPM, Bizagi Suite, the Oracle BPMS Suite, Sygnavio, or the new trend of open source offers like Camunda BPM among many others. Some of these platforms include the SOA Suite or rules engines, but some providers offer only environments for "Human Workflow"; i.e., they orchestrate processes with users, but not services with backoffice (SOA). While most of BPMS include process modelers, the reader must be clear that these components do not replace a BPA environment.

BPMS process modelers were designed for a process specification to be technically implemented, which is why they are very technical, but not good as analytical environments, or for businesspeople. Many BPMS vendors claim that their technological offer is universal, cutting through all layers and features, but they are not. BPMS are specialized environments for IT specialists, not for business users.

In summary, it can be concluded that there are many BPM application areas, and for each of these applications it is required a specialized tool to support the functionalities requested. There are many BPM tools, and the essential question is, with what purpose were they designed and what BPM area or specialty do they support?

1.7 Process Automation

To understand what automation involves, we will first describe a simple process of a manually organized credit application, to later explain how this process is nowadays technically implemented. The process starts with a credit application received by e-mail and then referred to a business executive in the bank. Through visual check, the executive reviews the application, and then he enters some data of the applicant in a risk analysis system. If the risk index is positive or acceptable, he enters the data application in a financial credit system and delivers the evaluated request to his superior for approval.

Automation of this process could be as follows: The credit application arrives via email and is scanned via an OCR (Optical Character Recognition); certain variables are extracted of the form and entered to a credit evaluation system. Then, an electronic document is created, which addresses the preparation of a work order in the process engine; this work order is sent to the executive's inbox. He selects from the list the proper application and displays the credit application in the process engine, reviews it formally and the process engine calls the risk analysis system through a web service, forwarding the relevant information (variables are transferred). If the analysis result is positive, the process engine automatically refers the approval request to his superior, entering the data into the financial credit system through a web service; finally, it is sent to his inbox for proper approval.

We could argue whether this process could be improved, but this case describes the difference between a manual and an automated process:

- If we talk about process automation, it does not mean that the process is fully automated.

- The principal component of the process automation is the process engine (control flow automation)

- The process engine controls the process through which users are guieded on what they need to do, as well as the result of their activities (human workflow management); It also controls internal and external interfaces with the systems involved in the process (services orchestration).

- The process engine makes the decisions on what type of activities or services must be called upon, through the technical logic implemented (technical process model) and the user's intervention points. Not always the implemented process logic has been mandatory; in certain circumstances, it may be influenced by the process participants, excepting that everything must be recorded.

Figure 11 show a generic representation of the process automation with a process engine.

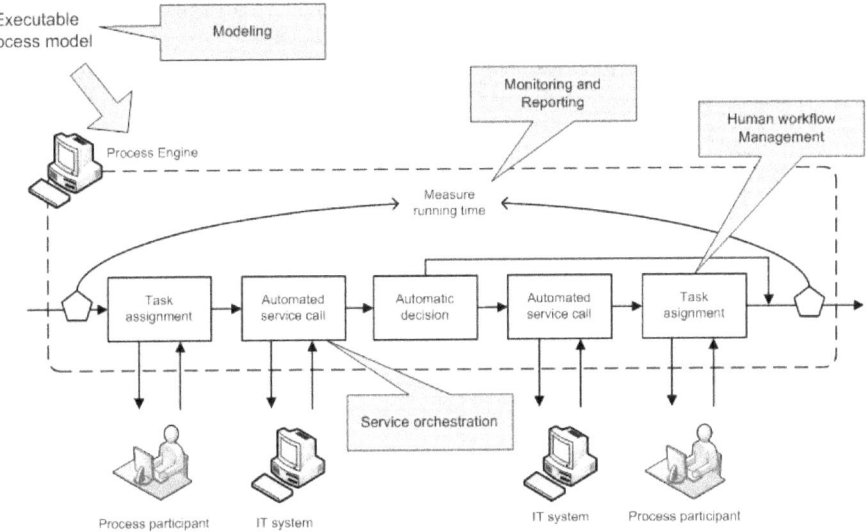

Figure 11 Automation of a process with a Process Engine, source: [1]

Multiple terms are used in literature and on the market for systems implementing processes: Workflow Management System (WfM), Business Processes Management Suite or System (BPMS), Workflow Engine and Process Engine. Usually, BPM Suite (BPMS) is the most comprehensive system that brings all built-in components (technical modeling, workflow engine, control panel, user interface, Application Programming Interface (API), and sometimes Enterprise Service Bus (ESB). The reader may assume that a process engine is an environment for developing the software that automates processes. Truly, it is a specialized development environment: It could be said that the workflow engine of the process engine is the flow compiler or interpreter, and that the technical model of the process represents the computer program code. Using the process engine environments has great advantages compared with the proper workflow development:

- The workflow engine specializes in interpreting and implementing the process logic, and therefore brings many functionalities that without it should be developed and tested before using them. That is, with a process engineer a BPM project is far more productive during the process implementation. However, a process engine cannot represent any functionality (that's why it is a specialized environment), and if required, they should be integrated into a system.

- A process engine has the capacity to integrate workflow management with business solutions (IT applications). In this way, they become powerful technical platforms, able to automate all kinds of processes from beginning to end, despite the technology that lies beneath, or the user's workplace. Some process engine platforms are even complemented by a bus or a service orchestrator, called Enterprise Service Bus (ESB), or other components, as a rule engine that increases flexibility of the environment.

- Since the process engine controls the process, it has absolute control over it, knows at all times where is every instance of each process that lives in it. The process maintains a detailed record of everything that has happened by using an event log. In this manner, it can keep indicators about on-line flow and real time, which serve as input for online processes controlling or Business Activity Monitoring (BAM). With a BAM, the management control can be integrated over the processes in real time.

These three features justify the use of a process engine, but there is also another very important benefit: The process engine works based on an executable process model designed by businesspeople. We are facing a shift of paradigm, in the sense of implementing a paper-based business process model, and this is precisely the aim of the new BPMN standard, notation to model processes.

1.8 Process Controlling

As described in previous sections, one of the primary goals of BPM is to improve effectiveness and efficiency of business processes aligned with the business strategy, contributing directly to increasing the corporation's business performance, in general. The information needed to control the process management is given by a concept of management that an organization should necessarily define, which in this work will be called "process-controlling".

The process controlling is a key factor to achieve the aims pursued with BPM. If monitoring of process controlling is insufficient, BPM will not lead to "the achievement of business objectives". Schmelzer [11] distinguishes between "strategic- and operational process-controlling".

Among the main strategic management control tasks, it can be listed:

- Planning of BPM strategic objectives, critical success factors and their measures. This planning could be the result of a "Process Balanced Scorecard"
- Control of the monitoring of strategic objectives, procedures and measures
- Identification and evaluation of strategic weaknesses
- Monitoring reports on the status of implementation of the strategy
- Coordination of corporate controlling with process controlling

The operational process controlling according to Schmelzer [11] covers the following tasks:

- Deduct the operational objectives from the process-oriented strategy
- Establish the metrics and indicators to measure the process performance
- Continuous measuring and monitoring of process execution
- Periodic behavioral and performance analysis of processes
- Monitoring reports on the results in operations process monitoring
- Coordination of operational process controlling with the business areas

From the tasks of operational management control recently listed, Schmelzer [11] infers the following rules:

1. Objectives must be defined for each business process, integrating them to a scorecard with metrics and indicators
2. The process objectives should be inferred from business objectives
3. The process performance should be constantly measured as well as the control and the degree of compliance with the objectives
4. The analysis process should be initiated if deviations are found outside the allowable ranges, aimed at discovering their causes and induce corrective measures
5. Periodic assessments must be coordinated for each business process to review the actual behavior
6. Responsibilities in the process and the management control cycle must be clearly specified

The concept of process controlling described by Schmelzer is equivalent to other concepts presented in literature. Online, and real time processes performance monitoring and measurement is called "BAM: Business Activity Monitoring".

The BAM has two main components:

- Records: BAM registers the variables that deliver process instances

- Measurement and calculation: records are evaluated, and defined indicators are calculated

If process management is one of the main objectives in BPM, then it is necessary to measure their performance in real-time. The famous saying "if you can't measure it, you can't improve it", also applies in BPM. Many BPM projects end with the automation of the business logic of a process, achieving greater control, and transparency regarding what is happening; but, if the implantation of a scorecard on the key management indicators is not considered, as well as a procedure able to allow the supervisor or process manager to take real-time action over the identified problems, it cannot be said that BPM is being used. BPM cycle closes with real-time Business Activity Monitoring (BAM).

Recording and measurement begins then, with Business Activity Monitoring cycle in operations. Indicators support us in answering to the question "What is happening?", but not necessarily respond to the question "How and why is it happening?" Scorecards, also called a cockpit as an analogy to the dashboard of an aircraft, which indicate us "what" is happening; also, alarm thresholds can be configured, which should provide warning signals only when we are out of the allowed range, but on a very few occasions the system can correct by its own the deviations detected. Usually, it is necessary an in-depth analysis process.

Suppose that a user has multiple process instances assigned, which are halted beyond allowed time, and not processed. Then, BAM triggers an alarm to the manager responsible for the process and informs him about the subject. The manager analyzes the situation and sees that the user took a medical leave. In that case, the manager can reassign these halted cases to another user and thus solve the problem. Another common example is when a user's workload exceeds his work capacity. The result is a bottleneck, and waiting time becomes more prolonged than expected. The process manager might request here, temporarily or permanently, additional resources, or easily reassign cases to another user. These simple cases can be resolved by operations, and thus optimizing the load and workload; in other cases problems are more complex and no answer can be given without going through an in-depth analysis phase. If the nature of problems is structural, it goes into a project of process redesign analysis, and if its cause is not found, it should pass to a process mining analysis.

Process controlling strives to deliver to its customers the so called value proposition. The value proposition has 4 elements, according to [Schmelzer08]:

1. Customer satisfaction: the external or internal client, is satisfied with the products and services delivered?
2. Quality is the degree of conformity between what was presented and what was actually received by the customer. Is the customer satisfied with what was demanded and promised?

3. Cycle times: Are cycle times of a process applicable with times expected by clients?
4. Cost is the price paid by consumer according to a product standard, and the price of the competition.

Customer satisfaction is for many organizations the most important indicator to measure the business process management. Customer satisfaction is conditioned, by two prerequisites:

- Assertive knowledge on customer requirements
- Services that meet customer's needs and necessities

First, the problems demand, objectives, intentions and desires of customers should be grasped and understood, in order to satisfy these demands. The responsibility of this task lies first in marketing and then in the products and services planning process. The organization must be understood as a gear, all gear parts should attempt the best coordination possible to achieve a satisfactory result.

It should be understood that none of the critical factors are independent, such us customer satisfaction, quality, delivery times or prices. They are all correlated, which is the reason why they are compared with a gear. Compared with a clock, if one part fails, it will affect the result, no matter how important the part is. If one of the parts does not work well, in a greater or lesser extent, the watch gains or loses time. In other words, secondary processes can play an important role in the supply of the value chain process (primary processes).

One of the most important critical factors of the BPM process-controlling concept is the continuous measuring and analysis of customer satisfaction. Periodic measurements might give some evidence of the weaknesses in the services that the organization is providing, but effectiveness is achieved by including in operations a permanent process performance measurement, and by the actions taken from measurements and analyzes carried out.

1.9 BPM Challenges and Benefits

Undoubtedly, the great challenge in using BPM is to continually improve the business proposal, offering higher quality services or new services that add value. For example, as the big internet companies show us every day, adding phone service on WhatsApp, taking instant video clips on Twitter, offering different access channels to self-service banking platforms, etc.

Other great challenges in our era towards digital transformation are:

- Take control in real time over automated organizational processes.
- Improve the logistics processes integrated into the organizational environment in time and quality.
- Enable integration and communication of physical devices (CPS) with IoT protocols.

Finally, if we introduce process-oriented management and apply the tools and methodologies that BPM offers us, we can achieve the following benefits:

- Improve understanding of what is done and how it is done
- Monitor and measure results
- Take control over business processes
- Reinforce and audit the "best practices"
- Reduce cycle times
- Reduce operating costs
- Improve performance
- Respond appropriately to changes in requirements

2 INDUSTRY 4.0: THE NEW AGE OF THE SMART INDUSTRY

We are facing a new industrial revolution, called "Industry 4.0". Number 4.0 indicates the transition towards "The Fourth Industrial Revolution". This was first presented by a group of researchers in 2011 at the Hannover Messe in Germany, one of the largest industrial fairs in the world.

According to this classification, we can name the following great stages since the beginning of the industrialization era:

Industry 1.0	1780 - 1870	Steam generation
Industry 2.0	1870 - 1950	Chain production, electrical energy
Industry 3.0	1950 - 2010	Higher level of automation, electronics and ICT
Industry 4.0	2010 - present	Cyber-Physical Systems (CPS), smart industry, Internet of Things (IoT), Big Data, hyper connectivity

Industry 4.0 represents a paradigm shift from "centralized" manufacturing and production to a "decentralized" but intelligent one. The new era indicates the transition towards the intelligent interconnection of machines and systems, not only on the production site itself, but also with the entire organizational eco-system. Unlimited potential opens in business process innovation, but also in all the ways in which society will interact globally. We are at the beginning of this new era and it will surely take place over a period of several decades. This industrial revolution will not only involve the company and its collaborators, but all interest groups and society in general.

Let's see some of the characteristics of Industry 4.0

2.1 Industry 4.0 and IoT

The fourth industrial revolution is characterized by incorporating:

- Smart services to manage your value chain and interoperability with all its external agents.

- Cyber Physical Systems (CPS), which are defined as a collaborative system of IT elements, designed to control physical electronic or mechanical devices.
- Internet of Things (IoT), which refers to connecting physical devices of any kind with IT systems, to manage and control the functionalities of the devices through the Internet protocol.

According to current data, 20 billion devices are expected by 2020 [12]. This high degree of connectivity means that business processes will be able to make more decisions in real time, because they are based on real data.

A manufacturing company (manufacturer of things) will have to develop IoT functionalities for its products. One of the functionalities that has been assigned greater importance is that of security. No one questions the value of having remote access to devices over the Internet. Surveillance systems can provide real-time alerts, vending machines can notify operators when replacement stock is reached. The Internet of Things should make life easier for users and companies by being connected and communicating with their devices, but as previously stated, it opens up great opportunities for "hackers"; a great challenge for the security industry.

2.2 Characteristics of processes in Industry 4.0

Unlike our current era in which automated processes deliver information to us in real time, the new industrial cycle is characterized by greater:

- autonomy in the administration of the links of a value chain,
- intelligence of the activities or devices responsible for decision-making,
- integration with all external agents that interact in the value chain and
- greater transparency in traceability and monitoring in production and logistics systems.

Let's look at a scenario that is already partially true and that was described by Schönthaler et al [13]. A business based on a collaborative business process and integrated with the Internet of Things (IoT).

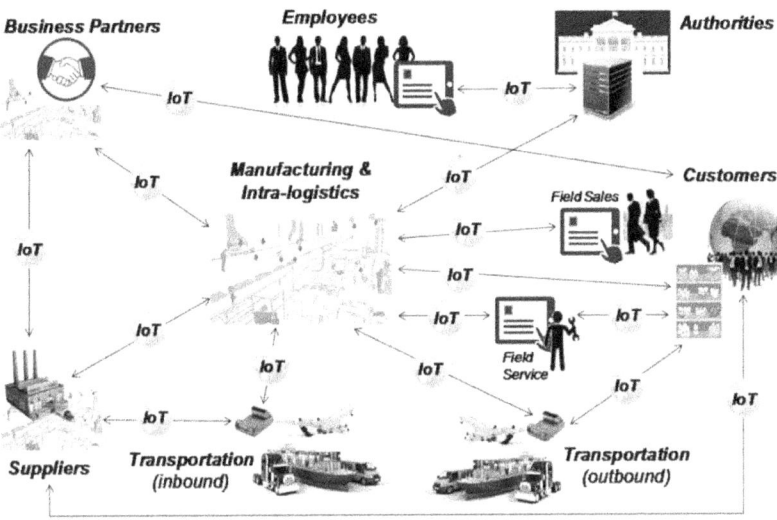

Figure 12 Scenario of a business in Industry 4.0 with IoT

Figure 12 shows a typical scenario that will be found in a few years later. You can see smart Cyber Physical System (CPS) devices connected to each other and with traditional IT systems but integrated with IoT services. The figure shows IoT-based communication throughout the value chain. The communication channels are integrated with all the actors, suppliers, business partners, government entities, employees, and distribution and transport logistics systems. Due to the degree of integration, the potentials for making supply chain management independent are enormous.

Thus, for example, the sales record, evaluates the inventory in real time and triggers, according to the programmed algorithms, the replacement of parts and materials with suppliers. In the same way, risk management processes, regulatory compliance, security aspects, etc. can be integrated. This type of production, business and real-time management is also called "smart factories".

The alarming increase in the speed of intelligent technological innovation in the last decade, will allow integrating "everything with everyone". Rifkin [14] describes how the internet network is expanding to create a new technology platform that connects everything to everyone, also called the "Internet of Everything (IoE)". Millions of sensors are connecting to resources, production lines, electricity and distribution networks, logistics networks, homes, offices, shops, vehicles, smartphones, etc.

2.3 Relationship exists between Industry 4.0 and BPM

Global economies tend more and more towards integration and standardization of services with their operators. Currently, the offer of standardized services in the cloud (cloud services) is huge and has matured a lot. Schönthaler et al further report that cloud services are "technically simple and inexpensive."

To achieve the integration and standardization of services, it is necessary to go through an earlier stage, the standardization of business or organizational processes. The reader might ask, where then is the competition concentrated? Would a price war to the death break out?

The answer, in part, is given by the authors Schönthaler et al. figure 13 shows that companies do not differ in the use of standardized services, but they do differ in the way they configure or design their business processes. So, the quality of service delivery will be very different between one competitor and another.

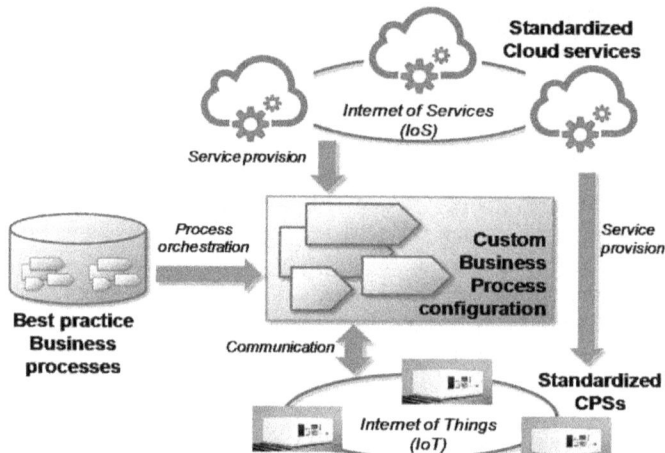

Figure 13 Customized business process orchestration

The highly competitive organizations will have to develop capacities of excellence in the understanding and management of their processes, in order to provide a greater degree of intelligence to the processes used in the links of the value chain. In addition to continuously improving the degree of business agility, that is, the ability to adapt to the changes required or desired (innovation), through its business processes.

The technological capabilities developed by Industry 4.0 allow through new digital platforms:

- Improve the business proposal, offering new services that add value. For example, add phone service on WhatsApp, take instant video clips on Twitter, offer different channels of access to self-service banking platforms, etc.
- Take control in real time over automated organizational processes.
- Improve the logistics processes integrated into the organizational environment in time and quality.
- Enable integration and communication of physical devices (CPS) with IoT protocols.

In this new era there is also a clear trend towards greater decentralization of processes, an observation that according to the authors Schönthaler et al leads to a new class of business processes, which they call "Business Process 4.0". However, it is still too early to predict the impact that these new technologies and tools may have on organizational processes.

2.4 Define the digital transformation strategy for your organization

If your business is not yet in the process of digital transformation, you will have to! That's how categorical MIT CISR (Massachusetts Institute of Technology) describes it in one of its monthly magazines. How to start? Most of the companies that started with this transformation process are in the initial stages and there are still no proven references that lead to a good design of digital platforms for an organization, but the MIT CISR identified three key factors [15]:

1. The organization must define how it wants to change its world
2. Identify the critical elements of the business
3. Define and design human-machine interactions

Somehow it will be necessary to express "a great vision" of how the lives of customers can be simplified and improved with the tools available for Industry 4.0. Companies like Amazon and Google demonstrate this daily. The speed of innovation in services is so great that we cannot capture the entire offer at the time it is made available. More traditional companies such as Philips Healthcare or John Deere are in the process of digital transformation by connecting their machines with IoT devices and offering real time monitoring and maintenance to their customers. For example, indicating parts changes, defect alerts and all the control of the functionality that can occur to the life cycle of an appliance. Philips declares "to be able to improve the quality of life of three billion people between now and 2025 [15]".

Regarding the second factor, Ross et al call for a break with the traditional paradigm of holding area managers or directors accountable in isolation for the execution of a strategic initiative, on the understanding that the sum of all the parties will give a positive result. Functional structures have the advantage of clearly delimiting responsibilities, but they have the great disadvantage that bureaucratic structures are installed that prevent efficient decision-making and make cross-coordination in organizational tasks and projects difficult.

The Industry 4.0 services are smaller, smarter and more comprehensive (smart services), therefore it is necessary to install new smaller but more flexible organizational units, equipped with business and technology people who work together for a common objective.

Digital transformation processes require the redefinition of organizational procedures towards the construction of business components; in the same way as the IT area transforms processes into digital services. In this way, organizations can reform their rigid (hierarchical) structures, without losing the allocation of responsibility regarding deliverables.

Finally, the third critical factor named by Ross et al, refers to defining and designing the integral capacity required by the profiles and professional roles of the new era. The professional of today cannot be trained only with knowledge in his subject, he must also acquire technological skills and get used to the fact that the updating of permanent knowledge will be part of his professional profile. Currently or in the past, the IT department worked with the business area to manage the required technology and the HR department worked with the business area to manage people.

The paradigm shift is that in this new era of Industry 4.0, it is necessary to form multidisciplinary teams that work around business components (services) and design human-machine interaction.

2.5 Examples of Best Practices in Digital Transformation

2.5.1 The Chilean Internal Revenue Service (SII)

The Chilean Internal Revenue Service (Servicio de Impuestos Internos SII) is an international example of successful digital transformation in most of its business processes [16].

The income tax return of main monthly tax returns and annual income of companies and individuals reaching the year 2019 over 99% online.

Services offered by the SII online

- Online electronic invoicing issue for independent professionals
- Online electronic invoicing issue for SMEs
- Simplified accounting proposal for SMEs
- Proposal and payment of monthly taxes
- Electronic Purchase and Sales Books
- Annual income statement for companies and individuals

Example of the 100% online VAT proposal process

As with Income, taxpayers can access a prefilled Proposal, to facilitate the declaration (income tax return) and monthly payment of the tax. The new tool is built with the information available in the purchase and sales registry, which automatically incorporates the electronic documents issued and received in the service.

With the incorporation of the new VAT Proposal, taxpayers can, on the same platform, issue and receive their tax documents, access their purchase and sales records, their proposed VAT debit or credit with or without movements, pay, rectify and postpone the pay.

Among the advantages offered by this new tool for taxpayers, the following stand out:

- Simplification of the VAT declaration and payment process
- Automatic generation of the Purchase and Sales Registry, exempting from the obligation to bring their Purchase and Sales Books to electronic invoice taxpayers

- Information inconsistencies between the VAT Form and the purchase and sales registry are avoided
- The declaration of the VAT tax credit is facilitated in those cases of loss of documents in the event of catastrophes, fires or other situations

Annual Award for Government Excellence 2018 and 2019

In 2018, the Internal Revenue Service was one of the winners of the Annual Award for Government Excellence, amount other government agencies.

This distinction, established to promote a culture of Business Excellence in public administration, is awarded annually by the Chilean Civil Service to three services that stand out for their results in the areas of efficiency and productivity, quality of service and people management.

In 2019 the SII received from the Chilean Club of CIO the award of the best Digital Transformation Project, with the introducing of the "Automatic VAT proposal process" in real time.

This award is a recognition of the management developed by the SII, marked by innovation at the service of people, and which is reflected in the daily work in support of taxpayers.

2.5.2 *Blockchain as a Service (BaaS) for Santiago Stock Exchange (Bolsa de Santiago)*

Being innovation a strategic pillar for the Santiago Stock Exchange, the incorporation of Blockchain technology is a natural step to facilitate the connectivity experience of customers, create new business models and thus promote the process of digital transformation [17].

Generating the best conditions for the stock and financial business, with innovative and world-class solutions, is one of the biggest challenges that the Santiago Stock Exchange has set itself.

The digital transformation has already significantly reduced the times and costs of the processes associated with the short sale of shares.

Along these lines, in 2018, it developed the first Blockchain application for a new version of the short sales and securities loan system, in order to reduce the time and costs of business processes. This made the Santiago Stock Exchange the first stock market in Latin America to have a production application using this technology.

Since its launch, the times and costs of the business processes associated with the short sale of shares have been significantly reduced. Today, contracts materialize in less than 90 seconds, compared to more than four days previously.

The next step is to extend this network to a business grade, where different market institutions can develop multiple applications for the financial market. For this, the Santiago Stock Exchange invited market partners to build a Technology Consortium for the development of a business platform (BaaS) that allows the creation of various software applications or systems based on Hyperledger Fabric technology from the Linux Foundation.

The Santiago Stock Exchange is the first Ibero-American stock exchange to have such an initiative.

International experience is showing that the creation of a consortium of these characteristics is associated with business excellence models developed by market infrastructures or associations of company's "hubs" for business relationships that are market leaders.

This is the case of the ASX the Australian Stock Exchange, DTCC the securities depository in the USA and SIX the Swiss Stock Exchange in Europe, to name a few cases in the financial industry; as well as the Maersk and IBM joint Venture for Trade Lens for the "Blockchain Shipping Solution" or Walmart for the "food traceability Solution". These infrastructures are currently promoting the digital transformation process and reducing operating costs by streamlining old process flows.

2.5.3   An example for e-Government: Estonia

Estonia's quest for digitization began in 1991, after the breakup of the Soviet Union. It had a clean slate and was not wedded to bureaucratic legacy systems that encumber so many countries. A country where internet access has legally been a human right since 2000 (www.e-estonia.com) [18].

Estonia started with e-Governance is a strategic choice for Estonia to improve the competitiveness of the state and increase the well-being of its people, while implementing hassle free governance. Citizens can select e-solutions from among a range of public services at a time and place convenient to them, as 99% of public services are now available to citizens as e-services. In most cases, there is no need to physically attend the agency providing the service. The efficiency of e-Government is most clearly expressed in terms of the working time ordinary people and officials save, which would otherwise be spent on bureaucracy and document handling [19].

In 2015, Estonia became the first country to offer e-residency, a program permitting citizens of other countries to become residents of Estonia without even needing to visit the country in-person. Through e-residency, foreign nationals become an Estonian digital citizen. By completing a simple registration process, e-residents can register a company, file taxes, and use all other services available to local Estonian citizens. The vision is to provide secure and effective digital services for global citizens who are investors, entrepreneurs, students, freelancers, and others, allowing them to contribute to the Estonian digital society and economy. (The 2017 Digital Evolution Index).

Estonia has become a great benchmark for many countries around the world. The digital transformation in all the government services makes a clear example on how you can improve the services to the citizens, reduce cost (paperless) and increase the quality of all government processes.

2.6 Industry 4.0 Challenges for BPM and e-Commerce

No one can deny that we are now facing a process of digital transformation transition to digitalization in nearly all the services of our globalized economy. How can this phenomenon be understood from an organizational perspective? The transition to digitalization is not only about switching from paper to the electronic environment, but it also affects the governance of the entire organizational ecosystem. This means that all processes of the value chain should be integrated with IT [3].

If this new industrial revolution digitalizes all logistic, purchase and sales processes, then e-commerce will account for over 90% of global commercial transactions [20]. In other words, business process and e-commerce cannot be managed in isolation anymore: behind every service there will be digitalized processes integrated with the entire business participant network.

The new industrial revolution will have a strong impact on the relation of BPM and e-Commerce because it moves manufacturing and production from a centralized to a decentralized paradigm. This will require a widespread adoption of smart interconnection of machinery and systems, not only at the same production site but also across the entire organizational ecosystem. An enormous potential opens for innovation in business processes and in the way, society interacts at a global level.

Thus, for example, records generated by selling processes allow real-time inventory assessment to trigger restocking of parts and materials from suppliers. Purchase orders, invoicing and payments processes can be automated with smart contracts and certificates that use blockchain technology [21], which has gain notoriety by underlying Bitcoin but is quite useful as a tamper-proof high-availability distributed ledger.

A big challenge when integrating the entire value chain, according to the Industry 4.0 concept, is the monitoring of processes' KPI's in real time them into a Corporate Balanced Scorecard that reflects strategic objectives. This is hard because in most organizations, BPMS (BPM Systems) and BI (Business Intelligence) analytical processes operate in isolation, as Vukšić et al. [22] show clearly. There are still big conceptual gaps between business intelligence (BI) more focused on data and process intelligence (BPMS and Process Mining) more focused on control of events.

The increasing speed of smart technology innovation over the last decade will soon allow integrating *everything with everyone*. The internet is expanding to create a new technological platform to this end, also known as the "Internet of Everything" (IoE) [14]. Billions of sensors are being connected to resources, production lines, electricity and distribution networks, logistic networks, homes, offices, stores, vehicles, smart phones, etc. These devices are at the *edge* of the Internet [9], sitting astride between the world of IT (Information Technologies) and the world of devices and OT (Operational Technologies).

The construction, maintenance and operation of the Industry 4.0 ecosystem raises huge challenges, but e-commerce brings to the table tools and techniques that allow to exploit a key aspect: from a BPM perspective, payment transactions are just functions within the logic of a business process, and almost all business services are associated with payment transactions that must be managed online and in real time.

3 CONTINUOS IMPROVEMENT TOOLS AND TECHNIQUES

A continuous improvement process, as the name implies, has no end to it. In contrast, improvement routines are expected to be integrated into the organization's daily activities and used to generate results in line with the firm's strategic objectives. The most prominent examples, such as the Toyota Production System, are stable and facilitate the spread of practices through the company [23].

Managers of any organization play a crucial role in the success of continuous improvement tools and techniques. Without the leadership, commitment and involvement of senior management, a continual improvement programmed is unlikely to be successful. We had been seeing organizations without clear understanding of continuous improvement plan and in few years, they have a lack of commitment to make this sustainable in the long run.

Continuous improvement is even more effective if it is introduced into an organization that has a learning culture. It is important to know and understand the culture of an organization. This will help identify what needs to be changed to promote continual improvement.

Creating a culture of quality requires fundamental changes in thinking and in practice, not to mention a lot of hard work. It means trusting and valuing employees to do the right thing and be empowered to generate innovative solutions to problems, even if it means they fail from time to time. It is only after creating a culture of quality within an organization that you can guarantee sustainable success throughout the life of your business.

3.1 PDCA: The Deming Cycle

The PDCA concept usually refers to the famous administrator who popularized it: William E. Deming. But in fact, the PDCA concept (or cycle) emerged in the 1930s, designed by American Walter Andrew Shewhart. Dr. William E. Deming was responsible for its widespread circulation which eventually got the concept to Japan where it was applied in businesses there. The PDCA cycle (short for plan, do, check, act) provides you with a systematic approach to testing different ideas and hypotheses. It can help you to implement continuous improvement throughout your organization using a structured framework. Although the steps proposed by the PDCA seem simple, the truth is that the success of this methodology lies in the promotion of engagement and fluid communication between all stakeholders.

PDCA is an acronym that gives name to a tool used in process quality management. Its focus is to solve problems by following the four phases. Because it's a cyclical tool, it also promotes continuous process improvement. To perform these steps in an effective manner, other quality tools can be required to be used. These quality tools can help mainly to analyze the problem and define the actions to be implemented [24].

The PDCA cycle ensures two types of corrective action – temporary and permanent. The temporary action is aimed at practically tackling and fixing the problem. The permanent corrective action consists of investigation and eliminating the root causes and thus targets the sustainability of the improved process [25].

Several authors state that the PDCA cycle is much more than a simple lean manufacturing tool. Instead, they mention that the PDCA cycle is a philosophy of continuous processes improvement introduced in the organizational culture of companies that is focused in the continuous learning and the knowledge creation.

In many organizations, management systems concepts are already incorporated into many existing programs, such as quality management. Our recommendation it´s first to understand that The Deming's cycle is more than just a quality tool. It´s a fundamental concept of continuous improvement processes embedded in the organizations culture.

PDCA is nothing more than a strategy focused on helping organizations (public and private) to achieve a true culture of excellence, where all the processes that companies execute provide maximum benefit.

3.2 Six Sigma

Six Sigma is a continuous improvement methodology that was developed by Motorola in the 80's with the goal of improving the quality of products and services based on a statistical concept of quality management aimed at reducing errors in the production process of a manufacturing company.

The main objective of Six Sigma is to plan and manage processes, so process results will have a minimal variation, improving their average performance without errors. The objective of the Six Sigma method (6 sigma) is to statistically achieve 3.4 errors or defects per one million events or opportunities (DPMO) [26]. The measuring system is based on the unit "error per one million opportunities" and the variation. It is understood as an error when the result "measured through the proper indicator" of the process is outside the acceptable range or targeted performance.

> PMO is the acronym for Defects Per One Million Opportunities. Measuring of a process efficiency means Defects Per One Million Opportunities and is calculated using the following formula: DPMO = (1,000,000 x number of defects) / (No. of units x number of opportunities). Where: Number of defects, is the number of units or nonconformities out of specification found in a certain number of units taken as a sample. Number of units, is the number of sample parts or elements produced. Number of opportunities, the number of possible defects within a single part or unit. Source: Wikipedia».

It is a very ambitious goal to get 3.4 defects per one million opportunities. A process efficiency can be classified based on its sigma level [26]:

- = 1 sigma = 690.000 DPMO = 69% error rate (31% efficiency)

- = 2 sigma = 308.538 DPMO = 30,8% error rate (69,2% efficiency)

- = 3 sigma = 66.807 DPMO = 6,7% error rate (93,3% efficiency)

- = 4 sigma = 6.210 DPMO = 0,62% error rate (99,38% efficiency)

- = 5 sigma = 233 DPMO = 0,02% error rate (99,98% efficiency)

- = 6 sigma = 3,4 DPMO = 0,00003% error rate (99,9997% efficiency)

If the Six Sigma goal could be achieved, the quality of results that would be achieved in the production would be without error 99,9997%; i.e., mathematically, a production curve that asymptotically tends to perfection, or to put it in another way, products, and services with almost no defects or faults. Obtaining 3.4 defects per one million opportunities is a fairly ambitious but achievable goal. Motorola reached at 1991, 6 Sigma [11]. In practice, this means that the prospects of significantly improving the results are unlimited.

It comes to pass that in the course of achieving a Six Sigma performance, or having already attained it, changes the specifications for acceptance (requirements) of the product or service, so what was once six sigma, today might not be, so new improvement efforts will be taken to achieve the six sigma level. Often, this is a consequence of the market conditions; what was once acceptable to customers, might not be today, so we progressively find more demanding customers, either by proper action, competition, or comparison with other industries.

The Six Sigma method, known as DMAIC (Define - Measure - Analyze - Improve - Control), consists of the application of a five phase-structured task that usually does not survive more than 90 days:

1. Define the problem (Define)

2. Observe and assess the problem (Measure)

3. Break down the problem (Analyze)

4. Act on the causes (Improve)

5. Analyze the results and standardize best practices (Control)

The definition of potential projects is identified in the first phase, in the framework of a portfolio analysis, which should be evaluated by its potential for improvement. The selected projects are prepared, and the team is trained by assigning the required priority, according to the "degree of difficulty" in the implementation, and the "impact on the customer satisfaction" [11].

The measurement phase consists on the delineation of the process, identifying the key customer requirements, outcome variables, as well as the input parameters that affect the process performance and key variables. From this characterization, it is possible to define the measuring system, and to measure the process capability.

In the third phase of analysis, the team analyzes data from current and historical events. The scenarios on the possible cause-effect relationship are developed and tested by using applicable statistical tools. In this way the team confirms the determinants of the process; i.e., the key input variables affecting the process response variables.

In the improvement phase, the team intends to determine cause-effect relationship (mathematical relationship between input variables and response variables of interest) to predict, improve, and optimize the process performance. Ultimately, it is determined the operational scope of the input parameters or process variables.

The final phase, control, consists of designing and documenting the controls necessary to ensure that the Six Sigma project achievements remain after changes have been implemented. Once the goals have been achieved and the mission is regarded as completed, the team reports to the direction and dissolves.

Conceptually, Six Sigma project results are supported by two approaches. The projects achieve on the one hand, to improve the characteristics of the product or service achieving higher incomes; on the other, cost savings derived from reducing gaps or errors, and shortening the process cycle time.

Roles in a Six Sigma project

The structure of roles in a Six Sigma project consists of:
- Champions: These are the business owners who decide which projects shall be carried out, define the strategy and arrange the resources needed for the project implementation.
- Masters (Master Black Belt): Experienced and capable staff of Six Sigma who have developed Black Belt activities, and coordinate, train, and manage Black Belt experts in their development as Six Sigma experts.
- Black Belt: Project managers and experts, generally working full time to the Six Sigma methodology. They lead projects and support in maintaining a culture of process improvement. They are responsible for the Green Belt training.
- Green Belt: Technical experts partially engaged (approx. 20%) in Six Sigma projects. They focus on different Six Sigma daily activities but participate or lead projects to attack problems in their areas.
- Yellow Belt: Business Expert who has Six Sigma basic knowledge. Username password that can provide improvement recommendations and assist in Six Sigma projects.

The experiences of companies that have decided to implement Six Sigma, allow to indicate: from aggregate figures of 90 per 100 reductions of the cycle time, or 15 billion dollars of savings in 11 years (Motorola), productivity gains of 6 per 100 in two years (Allied Signal), until the most recent, between 750 and 1,000 million dollar savings in a year (General Electric)

Nowadays Six Sigma is a continuous improvement method widely used worldwide in all spheres. This method, born in the industry with the aim of improving product quality in the manufacturing field, is being currently practiced in the U.S. mainly by services organizations rather than manufacturing companies, but it should be remarked that very few companies have reached the Six Sigma level [11].

Six Sigma is a continuous improvement technique that as others, if used, should be integrated with BPM. The reader will find more information on official pages of SixSigma.us and iSixSigma organizations dedicated to this discipline, methodology, training and certifications.

3.3 KAIZEN

Kaizen originates from a Japanese management philosophy of total quality, whose primary objective is the mastery of production process through continuous improvement, focusing primarily on people's skills [27] (Kaizen and Gemba are registered trademarks of Kaizen Institute, Ltd.). Suárez defines it in his book called "The Kaizen", as the philosophy of Continuous Improvement and Incremental Innovation, behind the "Total Quality Management" [28].

Kaizen can be translated from the Japanese as "Kai = change" and "Zen = the good". In a figurative sense, it can be interpreted as "change for better"; the common use of this translation to English would be "continuous improvement". The Kaizen philosophy conceives errors and problems as small "treasures" hiding improvement opportunities and innovation potentials. To put it another way, if problems transparency is not evidenced, improvements cannot be deducted. In that sense, it is a methodology of individual and collective work.

- "How can we do the job better tomorrow, then we're doing it today?" [27], is the core of the Kaizen's philosophy, 'not a single day can pass without any improvement'. So, the principle means that is always possible to make things better. In a seminar on October 2013, in Santiago, Chile, Masaaki Imai presented the core principles of the KAIZEN philosophy:

    - Improvements every day
    - All cooperators make improvements
    - Improvements in every place of the company, and in life

- From small incremental improvements to dramatic strategic improvements

Kaizen seeks to focus its efforts in creating "a flow lean in the workplace (operations) ". Optimization is conducted in the "Gemba (workplace) ". In the Kaizen concept, the flow lean intends to eliminate the activities that do not add value (muda=waste), and to minimize those activities that are unnecessary or do not contribute with added value.

From the BPM perspective, the Kaizen's basic principle says that the efforts should be focused on capturing the demands and requirements that create customer value. The improvement is aimed at both the internal and external clients (the client is king!); what is useful to the client, has "value". Kaizen considers the next steps of a process as an activity addressed to the client, and the preceding step, to the supplier. Each user participating in the process is identified as an internal supplier and as a client, simultaneously. He is committed to deliver the products and services to his customers, according to the quality requirements and times of delivery. The stakeholders of the continuous improvement are the people in all the levels of the organization, equally. Kaizen's success depends strongly on the people involved who are applying their expert knowledge and capacities. People must work in groups (teams), applying and sharing knowledge, analyzing in an open manner; they should also propose improvements as a work team and take responsibility over their decisions. The work team acts as small autonomous companies within the organization. They plan, analyze, take decisions, implement improvements, and communicate independently with their suppliers and clients. Therefore, the decision-making processes inside the organization are simplified and shortened. The top-level leaders may focus on performing their actual role, the strategic management.

The Kaizen-teams are shaped according to the cutting of sub-processes in a production chain or business process; they also have a series of methodologies and tools to conduct their analysis processes; for example:

5-S principles

Continuous improvement is a vital service to ensure the sustainability of management systems and the improvement of the performance of any business. 5S is a system for organizing spaces so work can be performed efficiently, effectively, and safely. This system focuses on putting everything where it belongs and keeping the workplace clean, which makes it easier for people to do their jobs without wasting time or risking injury. 5S began as part of the Toyota Production System (TPS), the manufacturing method begun by leaders at the Toyota Motor Company in the early and mid-20th century, aims to increase the value of products or services for customers. This is often accomplished by finding and eliminating waste from production processes.

5S involves assessing everything present in a space, removing what's unnecessary, organizing things logically, performing housekeeping tasks, and keeping this cycle going. Organize, clean, repeat. We had been seeing very successfully 5s programs in many manufacturing companies as well services organizations like banks, retails, hospitals, etc. I remember my first time visiting the company Aceros AZA in Chile and how well deployed was the 5S program. Everyone was involved to 5s in daily basis and it was part of the DNA of the entire organization.

These principles involve 5 Japanese words that start with an "S". Each expression has a significant meaning for the creation of an organized, clean and safe workplace:

- Seiri: Classify (to keep tidy, dispose what is not needed)

- Seiton: Organize (One place for everything and everything in its place)

- Size: Tidiness (to keep tidy the workplace, equipment and prevent the disorder)

- Seiketsu: Maintain (personal sense of order, discipline, and commitment)

- Shitsuke: Standardize (to establish habits based on the preceding 4 S')

The five "S" are the foundation of the concept of industrial productivity created in Japan; however, these principles are not representative of the Japanese culture, but they have successfully implemented it in the organization as a systematic application of the production flow.

The rules of 8-V

The aim of keeping the 8-V rules is to minimize the waste (muda) in:

As the reader might have realized, Kaizen intends not to neglect any detail; namely, it pursues excellence. Even the smallest mistake to be found has primary importance and, if it has not yet been found, the challenge for every individual is to search a potential for improvement, even if it is microscopic. The concept rewards the individual or the group that finds a mistake, or a potential for improvement; there is no debate whether it is profitable or not to solve the problem or introducing the improvement. The philosophy expects improvement contributions, and if these do not occur from time to time, we are not living the Kaizen philosophy.

- Inventories
- Transport
- Overproduction
- Waiting times
- While executing an activity
- Unnecessary movements
- Failures and its corresponding repair
- Unused employees' potential

Kaizen adopted also some western methodologies of quality, as the PDCA cycle already explained. The USA provided great support to Japan, after the Second World War to rebuild their industry, which consisted in the transfer of knowledge in statistic methods of process quality control. As we mention before the PDCA cycle is a systematic instrument for implementing and achieving the objectives that are pursued with Kaizen.

These methodological knowledges were conducted by W. Edwards Deming and Joseph M. Juran and was well assimilated by the Japanese. This mix of emotional intelligence of the Orientals, and the rational intelligence of the Westerns, caused what is now known as the Kaizen total quality concept. The implementation of this strategy in the Japanese industry led the nation to become as one of the principal economies in the world.

The following will summarize the general principles of Kaizen. The reader interested in further examination, may recur to the already-mentioned literature, or to the Kaizen Institute, Ltd. Organization.

Here are the conditions for the generation of the Lean-Kaizen flow:

- Implementing the 5S
- Standardization
- Visual management
- MUDA elimination
- Reorganize the management structure
- Build a KAIZEN culture

Kaizen general principles

- Process-oriented, rather than result-oriented
- Integrating all the stakeholders of a production or service chain
- Commitment of the top-management levels
- An efficient vertical and horizontal communication, without hindrance
- Continuous improvement in all the products and processes, internal and external
- The customer is king
- Investment in staff
- The quality management starts and concludes the training stage
- Two heads are better than one
- Everyone participates in the determination and communication of the goals

3.4 Lean Management

In the decade of the 80's the japanese automakers (especially Toyota) drew attention in western countries, realizing japanese quality and efficiency. Statistics showed that Japanese vehicles were less likely to have car failures, offering multi-year guarantee, and therefore, they endured a great deal longer than European or American cars. It was also stressed that every time Toyota showed an apparent weakness and appeared vulnerable to competitors, it improved miraculously and came out stronger. What was the secret of the Japanese manufacturers? The secret of their continuous improvement was later transformed into the concept of "Lean Management". The book "The Toyota Way" [29] explains the production system and the management style that Toyota applied, which reveals how this strategy obtained differentiating advantages in the marketplace:

"The key of the Toyota model, and what made Toyota success something unique, were not its individual elements, but having all these elements together in a single system. This should be practiced every day very consistently and not in sprints".

Maybe the best-known part of the lean system, is that about the process management seeking perfection. For Toyota, the right process will produce the correct results, and going still further, Toyota prefers a bad manager managing a right process than a good manager managing a bad process.

"We could say that the basic secret of TPS is establishing continuous-flow processes, bringing problems out into the open....... When problems arise, the TPS advocates for a halt the processes so as to solve the problems, and to achieve a good quality in the first place, which is as a way of thinking that seems far removed from conventional management. The reflection (Hanseai), and the continuous improvement from working groups (Kaizen), must figure out the problems; it is important that improved methods be standardized to guarantee that they will operate accordingly thereafter".

The Lean Management methodology arises from the need to eliminate unnecessary steps in the production chain, controlling primary activities, and giving control to the individual that does the job, as support to the value chain. This is, as its name clearly indicates, the direction whereto it is headed: "Lean or agile Manufacturing".

Its greatest contribution is that when it is properly applied, costs are reduced; in addition, processes are improved and waste is eliminated, which is translated directly into the enhancement of customer satisfaction and maintenance of profit margin. Like any methodology, its principles are the key to carry it out successfully, which aims to the following [30]:

1. The perfect quality first: That is, the search for zero defects, identification and resolution of problems at their source, thus avoiding the difficulties that could affect the production process. Therefore, the identification of the entire value stream for each product is so important; specifically, the value stream analysis shows almost always three types of actions along it. Before continuing with the production steps, many other steps will be discovered, whose value creation is unambiguous; many other steps that do not create any value will be found as well, which are unavoidable according to current technology and available production assets; and then, it is possible to discover additional steps that do not create any value and can be avoided immediately.

2. Minimizing waste: This refers to the elimination of all activities with no value-added and safety network, and the optimization of the use of scarce resources such as capital, human resources and space. A continuous flow and a more efficient operation help for things to work better when focused on the product and needs, rather than in the organization or the machinery, so that all the activities necessary to design, request and provide a product are made in a continuous flow.

3. Continuous improvement: It aims at reducing costs, improving quality, increasing productivity, and sharing information among members of the production group. It searches for excellence in the product, and to achieve this, it is essential to enhance transparency; all those who are involved in

the process, as subcontractors, first-tier providers, system integrators, distributors, consumers, employees, can see everything; thus, it is easier to find better methodologies for value creation.

4. Pull processes: This means that products are thrown, i.e., requested by the end-customer, not pushed by the end of production, to ensure the total satisfaction of those who requested the product. To accomplish this, it is necessary to design, program and do exactly what the consumer wants, and when he wants, leaving the customer being the one who pulls the product according to his needs, rather than pushing products, often unwanted, to the consumer.

5. Flexibility: This aims at the ability to quickly produce different combinations of a wide range of products, without sacrificing efficiency due to lower production volumes.

6. Building and maintaining a long term relationship of trust with suppliers, making agreements of sharing risks, costs, and information; this could be defined as the lean thinking key concept; that is, the value of the product, which can only be installed by the end-customer, and is only significant when is expressed as a specific product that meets the customer's needs at a particular price, at a certain time.

The Toyota model has 14 principles, which are here under listed [29]:

1. Your management decisions should be based on a long-term philosophy, at the expense of what happens to the short-term financial goals
2. The right process will produce the right results
3. Use pull systems to avoid overproduction
4. Level out the workload. Work like the tortoise rather than the hare
5. Learn to stop, so as to solve the problems, and to achieve a good quality at first

6. Standardized tasks are the foundation for continuous improvement and worker's-training
7. Use visual controls, so as not to hide problems
8. Use only reliable and validated technology
9. Help leaders who understand thoroughly the work thrive; live the philosophy, and teach others
10. Develop the talents and teams who adopt the philosophy of the company
11. Respect your network of partners and suppliers, helping them to improve
12. Go see him for yourself to fully understand the situation (genchi genbutstu)
13. Make decisions slowly by consensus, having thoroughly considered all the options; deploy them quickly
14. Become an organization that learns through regular reflection (hansei) and continuous improvement (Kaizen).

4 BUSINESS EXCELLENCE FRAMEWORKS (BEF)

The last two decades have witnessed the increasing application of business excellence frameworks as more companies have learned how to use them and to obtain superior performances [31]. This increasing adoption of the Business Excellence Frameworks around the world, has been improving the performance of many organization in the public and private sectors.

Business Excellence, as described by the European Foundation for Quality Management (EFQM), refers to; "Outstanding practices in managing the organization and achieving results, all based on a set of eight fundamental concepts", these being, "results orientation; customer focus; leadership and constancy of purpose; management by processes and facts; people development and involvement; continuous learning, innovation and improvement; partnership development; and public responsibility".

Business excellence models are frameworks that, when applied within an organization, can help to focus thought and action in a more systematic and structured way that should lead to increased performance. Facing an increasingly turbulent and chaotic environment, more and more companies have implemented business excellence strategies and made quality a key element of their business philosophy as quality leads to improved business performance [32].

The value of the Business Excellence Framework is intentionally non-prescriptive. It does not tell leaders how to manage their organizations. In general, business excellence frameworks (BEF) have been developed by national bodies as a basis for award programs, like USA, Europe, Singapore, Philippines, Australia, New Zealand, UAE, Brazil, México, among others. For most of these bodies, the awards themselves are secondary in importance to the widespread take up of the concepts of business excellence, which ultimately lead to improved national economic performance and increase competitiveness. One of the most relevant examples are Singapore and UAE, because for more than 20 years both Business Excellence Awards had been helping government agencies to improve the performance and offer a better service to the citizens and stakeholders.

The criteria to evaluate whether an organization has achieved business excellence usually rely on quality award frameworks such as the European Quality Award, the Malcolm-Baldridge National Quality Award and the Singapore Quality Award, among others. Regardless of sector, size, structure or maturity, organizations need to establish an appropriate management framework to be successful. The Baldrige, EFQM, Singapore, Dubai Excellence Models is a practical, non-prescriptive framework that enables organizations to:

- Assess where they are on the path to excellence; helping them to understand their key strengths and potential gaps in relation to their stated Vision, Mission, Value Proposition, Mains Objectives, etc.
- Provide a common vocabulary and way of thinking about the organization that facilitates the effective communication of ideas, among all the stakeholders.
- Provide a basic structure for the organization's management system. These frameworks provide a holistic view of the organization and it can be used to determine how these different methods fit together and complement each other.

The Malcolm Baldrige National Quality Award, the Singapore Business Excellence Framework, the Australian Business Excellence Framework (ABEF) or the European Foundation for Quality Management (EFQM). These excellence business frameworks provide guidelines and criteria for evaluation and are used by companies across the world as groundwork for continuous improvement [33].

Business Excellence Frameworks are essentially assessment models. They are used to assess an organization's strengths and areas for improvement. From this information, senior leaders can make sensible decisions on the actions needed to achieve the desired results. BEF applies to all type of organizations. Achieving business excellence requires a concerted and systematically effort in many areas of the organization and with the support/sponsor of the top management. Developing business excellence is a manifestation of continuous improvements in all critical activities of the organization, and, it's the quest for excellence that will help in the long run to achieve recognition for the stakeholders and sustainable results.

Organizations assess their own system against the detailed material available (criteria for performance excellence, we will describe in this chapter Baldrige, EFQM, Singapore and Dubai). This works through the foundation criteria based on categories, which represent a collection of processes and represents outcomes.

4.1 The Malcolm Baldrige Framework

In the western world in early the 80s, appeared statistic approaches to improve control processes. So, came to life TQM (Total Quality Management) approach, based on a statistic management control, but its application requires of a rigorous discipline in the organization, which is difficult to reach.

Japanese companies, particularly Toyota, recognized at the beginning of the 90s, the shift to the demand markets, so they focused their management to the business needs (clients). Toyota developed the concept Toyota Production System (TPS) [29]. This was characterized by having a very plane organizational structure, installing multidisciplinary teams (MDT) on production centers with the task of solving in an autonomous manner proposal of continuous improvement in production processes.

This work system was also called Lean Production; this means, to remove fat to bureaucratic and slow organizational structures in their decision processes.

In the mid-1980's Japan was an economic power; on the other hand, the largest U.S. companies who were under great pressure, and bureaucratic, were forced to seek excellence in performance and innovation; otherwise, they risked to lose further competitiveness. The U.S. government instructed in 1981 its Commerce Secretary, Mr. Malcolm Baldrige, to seek a solution to respond to the Japanese challenge. Malcolm Baldrige invited the industry leaders throughout the USA to seek a solution and thus regain the country's competitiveness. The result of this work was the creation of a framework of excellence to measure and improve the integral management of organizations, called the "Malcolm Baldrige Model". This was finally materialized in a US Public Law 100-107, promulgated on August 20, 1987 as "Malcolm Baldrige National Quality Award".

In a Baldrige 20/20 [34] paper, Professor of Harward, Rosabeth Moss Kanter warns on the current situation of the US companies:

"Now, in 2011, U.S. competitiveness is again at risk, with a new set of Asian challengers from China and emerging market countries". The text continues: "This context makes the Baldrige Performance Criteria more necessary and appropriate than ever. Continuous improvement is not merely a good thing for a handful of companies, but a survival strategy for every organization, as the only way to create organizations capable of rapid adjustment to rising standards and changing conditions".

Given the high degree of competitiveness exerted on American companies in the global market, since the 1980's until today, the U.S. government is trying to motivate national companies through the Malcolm Baldrige National Quality Award, to use the framework to achieve a high-performance and high degree of competitiveness, internationally. This means that those companies that are located outside the U.S.A. cannot apply for this award. However, the Malcolm Baldrige Model is widely used as a reference framework by companies outside the U.S.A.; also adopted with certain modifications, as a quality national award in most countries. An example of this is the "Asia Pacific Quality Organization (APQO)", which was founded mid-1980 with the aim of promoting quality management in the Asia-Pacific region. This nonprofit organization uses as a reference framework, the Malcolm Baldrige Model to awarding the "Global Performance Excellence Award (GPEA)".

The Baldrige Award aims to:

- Reward and recognize the companies' achievements that improve the quality of their products and services

- Provide best practices for other companies, to improve their service performance
- Define guidelines and criteria that can be used in the assessment of the efforts with a view to improve quality
- Reduce the threat of external enterprises in the U.S. market, strengthening the national industry
- Promote the implementation of innovations, both in small and large companies

Baldrige Model Structure

The Malcolm Baldrige framework is basically based on the following principles and values, concepts that have been observed in high-performance organizations that successfully implemented them [35]:

- Leadership with visionary skills
- Client-oriented
- Organizational and personal learning
- Appraisal of employees and partners
- Business agility
- Long-term planning (future)
- Continuous improvement and innovation
- Management by facts
- Social responsibility
- Results and value creation approach
- Systematic perspective

These principles and values are set out in three large blocks that support the Baldrige framework structure (see figure 14):

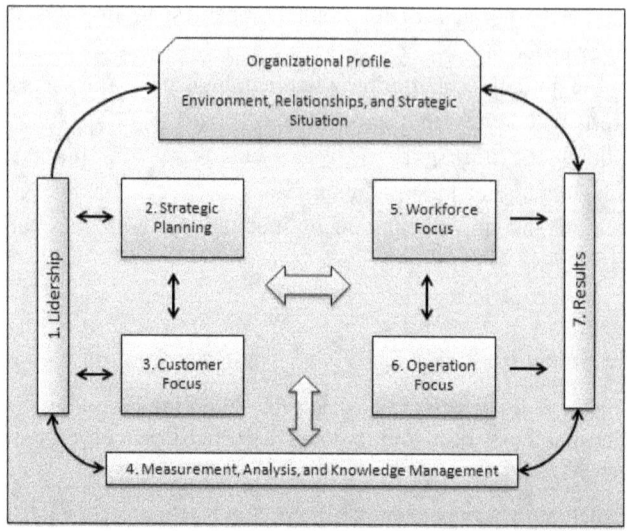

Figure 14 Baldrige Criteria for Performance Excellence Framework

- Organizational Profile
    - Relates to the context in which the organization operates, the relationship with the environment, the challenges and strategic situation, weaknesses and advantages, etc.
- Organizational Performance System: consists of six criteria, which are related under a structure of processes and results.
    - Leadership (1), Strategic Planning (2), Customer Focus (3), they represent the "Leadership" triad.
    - Workforce Focus (5), Operation Focus (6), and Results (7), they represent the "Results" triad.
- System Foundation
    - Measurement, Analysis and Knowledge Management (4), are fundamental processes to feed the virtuous circle of continuous improvement

Each of these criteria is subdivided into a series of sub-criteria (examination items), and in turn, each of these includes a series of areas (areas to address). Each sub-criterion has a maximum score, and by adding them up, the value of each criterion is obtained.

Assessment Process

The system of assessment to apply for the Baldridge Award is based on the response to the implementation of the criteria, segmented in two dimensions, "processes", and "results". The "processes" category refers to the methods that the organization uses to implement criterion 1 to 6; and the "results" category, to demonstrate the achievements obtained in the sub-criterion listed in category 7. It is worth mentioning that Baldrige demands for the "results" (7) category, five years of positive trends for each of the sub-criterion of results. Other assessment programs are less demanding, for example, the "National Quality and Excellence Management Award" in Chile demands 3 years of positive trend.

The evaluation structure, as seen in figure 15, is described in a document called "Criteria for Performance Excellence".

The Malcolm Baldrige excellence framework is built on a holistic and systemic view, with a strong emphasis on the causal and dynamic relationship between the leadership, the staff, and the results.

It is also important to mention that different specialized frameworks had been developed during the last decade for the Baldrige framework, by category. Originally, in 1987 the focus point was in the manufacturing sector, to later incorporating specialized frameworks for the sector of services, nonprofit organizations, public administration, Health, and education.

Nr	Categories	Points	Subcriteria	Points
1	Leadership	120	1.1 Senior Leadership	70
			1.2 Governance and Societal Responsabilities	50
2	Strategic Planning	85	2.1 Strategy Development	40
			2.2 Strategy Implementation	45
3	Costumer Focus	85	3.1 Voice of the customer	45
			3.2 Customer Engagement	40
4	Measurement Analysis, K-Mgnt	90	4.1 Measurement, Analysis and Improvement	45
			4.2 Knowledge Mgnt and IT	45
5	Workforce Focus	85	5.1 Workforce Environment	40
			5.2 Workforce Engagement	45
6	Operation Focus	85	6.1 Work Systems	45
			6.2 Work Processes	40
7	Results	450	7.1 Products and Process Outcomes	120
			7.2 Customer Focused Outcomes	90
			7.3 Workforce Focused Outcomes	80
			7.4 Leadership and Governance Outcomes	80
			7.5 Financial and Market Outcomes	80
	Total Points	1000		

Figure 15 Criteria for Performance Excellence

Established by the U.S. Congress to raise awareness of quality management, the Malcolm Baldrige National Quality Award (MBNQA) is awarded annually to organizations that prove passion for quality and obtain performance excellence. The Baldrige framework aims to help organizations to achieve excellence. It is based on several core values and concepts and provides the Baldrige Criteria for Performance Excellence that comprises seven critical areas. During the time these criteria have proved to constitute a "powerful set of guidelines for running an effective organization" [36].

The Baldrige framework is proven to bring about powerful changes in organizational performance and culture. Organizations using the Baldrige criteria are able to develop business resilience and an integrated focus on sustainable performance (NIST, 2015). This framework can be used to improve any part of your organization and to deliver some of the following benefits:

- Effective prioritization of your improvement efforts to deliver maximum benefits
- Process efficiency and effectiveness through reduced waste and variation
- Empowered and motivated workforce with increased retention

- Increased productivity and reduced operational costs
- Focus on customer service delivering superior perception of value
- Sustainable performance by increasing stakeholder value

Additionally, the Baldrige Framework provides an umbrella under which a number of business initiatives can be integrated to form one coherent, cohesive organizational systems model. Business initiatives that fit comfortably within the MBNQA include: Business Process Management, ISO 9001 series, Lean Management, Six Sigma, Balanced Scorecard, Risk Management, Safety Management and Great Place to work.

The Baldrige framework Core values and concepts (NIST, 2010):

- Systems perspective
- Visionary leadership
- Customer focused excellence
- Valuing people
- Organizational learning and agility
- Focus on success
- Managing for innovation
- Societal responsibility
- Ethics and transparency
- Delivering value and results

According to National Institute of Standard and Technology (NIST), the criteria are focused on two goals: "delivering ever improving value to customers and improving the organization's overall performance" [37].

4.1.1 Malcolm Baldrige Criteria (NIST, 2010):

1. **Leadership**: Senior leadership (the role of senior leaders, role-model senior leaders), Governance and societal responsibilities (organizational governance; legal compliance, ethics and risks, public concerns, conservation of natural resources, societal responsibility, community support).

2. **Strategy**: Strategy development (a context for strategy development, a future oriented basis for action, competitive leadership, work systems),

Strategy implementation (developing and deploying action plans, performing analyses to support resource allocation, creating workforce plans, projecting your future environment, projecting and comparing your performance).

3. **Customers**: Voice of the customer (customer listening, actionable information, listening/learning and business strategy, social media, customer and market knowledge, customers' satisfaction with competitors), Customer engagement (engagement as a strategic action, customer relationship strategies, brand management, complaint management).

4. **Measurement, Analysis, and Knowledge Management**: Measurement, analysis, and improvement of organizational performance (aligning and integrating your performance management system; the case for comparative data; selecting and using comparative data; reviewing performance; analyzing performance; aligning analysis, performance review, and planning; understanding causality), Information and knowledge management (information management, data and information availability, knowledge management, organizational learning).

5. **Workforce**: Workforce environment (workforce capability and capacity, workforce support), Workforce engagement (high performance, workforce engagement and performance, drivers of workforce engagement, factors inhibiting engagement, compensation and recognition, others indicators of workforce engagement, workforce development needs, learning and development locations and formats, individual learning and development needs, customer contact training, learning and development effectiveness).

6. **Operations**: Work processes (work process requirements, key product related and business processes, work process design, in-process measures, process performance, key support processes, process improvement, supply-chain management, innovation management), Operational effectiveness (cost control, managing cybersecurity, workplace safety, business continuity).

7. **Results**: Product and process results (measures of product performance, examples of product measures, product performance and customer indicators, process effectiveness and efficiency measures, measures of

organizational and operational performance), Customer-focused results (your performance as viewed by your customers, results that go beyond satisfaction), Workforce-focused results (workforce results factors, workforce capacity and capability, workforce engagement), Leadership and governance results (importance of high ethical standards, results to report, sanctions or adverse actions, measures of strategy implementation), Financial and market results (senior leaders' role, appropriate measures to report).

The Criteria, see figure 14, look at the linkages between the various elements of your business as shown in the diagram. Some examples of these linkages:

- The connections between your processes and the results you achieve.
- The need for data in the strategic planning process and for improving operations.
- The connection between workforce planning and strategic planning.
- The need for customer and market knowledge in establishing your strategy and action plans.
- The connection between your action plans and any changes needed in your operations.

The importance with these Criteria Characteristics are to:

- focus on results in all areas of performance to ensure all strategies are balanced,
- non-prescriptive and adaptable to promote creative and flexible approaches to foster incremental and breakthrough improvements,
- support a systematic perspective to maintain organization-wide goal alignment,
- support goal-based diagnosis based on a profile of performance orientated strengths and opportunities to improve.

The value is that Baldrige is intentionally non-prescriptive. It does not tell leaders how to manage their organizations. There are no two organizations alike – organizations operate in different environments, even in the same industry or market, are pursuing different strategies; they have different core competencies; and they are addressing different strategic challenges.

4.2 The EFQM Model

Soon after the appearance of the Malcolm Baldrige Model is born in Europe in the year 1988 the EFQM (European Foundation for Quality Management), with the support of the European Commission. The EFQM Model is based on the Edward Deming (Japan 1951), and Malcolm Baldrige (1987) Models.

The EFQM Model [38] is a standardized (reference) framework and a management model that seeks the stakeholder's satisfaction: Clients, People, Investors, Alliances, and Suppliers, agreeing with the environment through their People, Processes, Resources, Knowledge, and Technology.

The EFQM Model is the result of the general performance of an organization depends on the "Leadership" that conducts and drives the strategy, which is materialized through the "People", the "Alliances", and most important, their "Business Processes" control.

The EFQM Excellence Model is based on a set of European values, first expressed in the European Convention on Human Rights (1953) and the European Social Charter (revised in 1996). This treaty is ratified by the 47 member states of the Council of Europe and the principles are incorporated into national legislation. The Fundamental Concepts of Excellence build on the foundation of these basic human rights, assuming they are universally applied. Recognizing the role business can play in supporting the broader goals of the United Nations, the UN Global Compact (2000) was established. This initiative encourages organizations to actively apply these values, set out as 10 Principles for sustainable and socially responsible business, across their global operations. Whilst a number of these principles are explicitly covered in the EFQM Excellence Model, a number are implicit, including those relating to human rights, corruption, bribery and forced labour, as these are already a legal requirement within Europe (EFQM, 2017).

The EFQM Model, a globally recognized framework that supports organizations in managing change and improving performance, has experienced a number of improvement cycles over the years to make sure that it not only remains relevant but continues to set the management agenda for any organization wanting a long term, sustainable future (EFQM, 2013)

The EFQM proposes to "achieve success", that organizations need to establish a proper management system, independent of their category, size, structure, or maturity. The EFQM model rests on three main pillars, based on the concept of value for clients and stakeholders:

1. Fundamental Concepts of Excellence: Basic principles that establish the core foundations for an organization to achieve a sustained excellence.
2. EFQM model structure: A reference framework that helps to materialize the Basic Concepts.

3. RADAR Logic Scheme: Management Tool and dynamic scheme of assessment that supports the organization to face the challenges in achieving the sustained excellence.

In the following sections, we will introduce these three pillars.

4.2.1 Fundamental Concepts of Excellence

The Fundamental Concepts of Excellence describe guidelines and are the basis for any organization to achieve excellence sustained over time. The text description is in a language addressed to the top management. We will now summarize the guidelines of this concept.

Adding value for customers:

"Excellent organizations add a constant value for customers, understanding, anticipating, and satisfying the needs, expectations, and opportunities".

In a more detailed description we name both, the existing and potential clients; emphasis is placed on transforming the needs and expectations in value proposals, attractive for the clients; also to continue innovating in products and services, and constantly reviewing the client's perceptions, and finally, comparing the performance with relevant references.

Creating a sustainable future:

"Excellent organizations produce a positive impact in the world around them, because they increase their own performance, while improving the economic, environmental, and social conditions of the communities they are in touch with".

In a more detailed description, we can see how to interpret and promote the three economic, environmental, and social dimensions in which the organization operates.

Developing organizational capability.

"Excellent organizations increase their capacities by an effective change management, within and outside them".

In a more detailed description, we consider various factors, as requirements to attain the sustained development of the capacities in the organization. Among them, we find the need to develop an organizational culture based on the spirit of collaboration and teamwork; thus, the financial and technological resources can be ensured, establishing right networks to be able to identify opportunities of alliances to increase the added value to the stakeholders, among others.

Take advantage of creativity and innovation:

"Excellent organizations generate greater value and better results through continuous improvement and systematic innovation, taking advantage of the creativity of their stakeholders".

In a complete description, we can mention various initiatives promoting and fostering the creativity to innovate, to innovate approaching all stakeholders equally. It also mentions the importance of supporting the initiatives with proper resources, testing and accomplishing the ideas within reasonable time limits.

Leading with vision, inspiration, and integrity:

"Excellent organizations have leaders that shape the future and make it real, acting as a reference model of their ethical values and principles".

In a more detailed description, we can observe the capacities and abilities that a leader must develop to conduct with vision, inspiration, and responsibility. These include the principles of delegation, social responsibility, ethical behavior, transparency, and integrity, among others.

Managing with agility:

"Excellent organizations are recognized generally, by the ability they have to identify and respond efficiently and effectively to opportunities and threats".

In a more detailed description, we can observe the capacities to develop that organizations need to achieve business agility; that is, the capacity to adapt to the changes of the environment through their processes and change management.

Succeeding through the talent of people:

"Excellent organizations value people that integrate them and create a culture of delegation and assumption of responsibilities, making possible the achievement of both, the personal objectives and those of the organization's".

In a more detailed description, we find first, all the necessary competencies that people require to support the achievement of the strategic objectives; and, second, the respect for people's diversity, and to a healthy balance between life and work.

Sustaining outstanding results:

"Excellent organizations achieve outstanding results, sustained over time, and satisfy the needs of all their stakeholders in the short and long-term, in the context of their operating environment".

In a more detailed description, we can depict the several necessary actions for the organization to develop the capacity to permanently evaluate and analyze the results achieved. Thus, the market trend can be followed without losing the competitiveness levels and high levels of confidence of the stakeholders.

4.2.2 EFQM Model Structure

The EFQM model structure is formed by nine criteria and thirty-two sub-criteria. These nine criteria are divided into two large blocks called enablers (facilitating agents), or capacity developments that cover the first five criteria (leadership, people, strategy, partnership & resources, and processes); the rest of their four criteria are result-oriented (people results, customer results, society results, and business results). Figure 16 shows the EFQM model structure (2013).

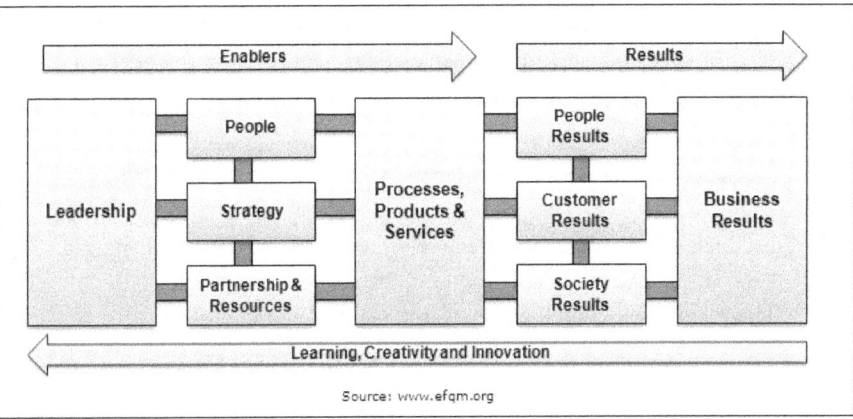

Figure 16 EFQM Model Structure (2013)

The first block (enablers) describes the organization's duty (the processes), and the second block, the organization's achievements (the results). The excellence model is embedded in a circle of continuous improvement, as we will see below. It is also noteworthy that processes play an important role within the block of facilitating agents, because it is through the processes that their products and services have the greatest effect on the main criterion of the second block, "The customer results". The process management had also a direct and positive relationship with the leadership, strategy, and the people. That is, the BPM discipline supports largely the monitoring for the achievement of the objectives to be pursued through the excellence models; therefore, and according to the author, it becomes a key factor to achieve excellence.

The main criteria of the EFQM model structure (2013) are divided in sub-criteria, reaching a total of 32, and these have several additional elements and examples that are useful to better understand the meaning of these criteria. The structure diagram shows in the block edges, some arrows indicating the model dynamic nature; this includes the development of the capacities through enablers, operation's measuring results, to the learning and innovation. This optimizes the performance of the enablers, entering by that into a virtuous circle of continuous improvement.

Following, and as an example, we will cite the definition of the two important criteria of the EFQM version, mainly those that are directly related to BPM (the interested reader may obtain a description of the model in print or digital formats, through the web site www.efqm.org).

Criterion: Processes, Products and Services

Definition

"Excellent organizations design, manage and improve processes to generate increasing value for customers and other stakeholders".

- Processes are designed and managed to optimize the value for stakeholders
- Products and Services are developed to provide an optimal value to the clients
- Products and Services are effectively promoted and put on the market
- Products and Services are produced, distributed, and managed
- The relationship with the clients are managed and improved

In the model description, we find examples in each of these sub-criteria, as cited hereunder:

"Processes are designed and managed, to optimize the value for the stakeholders":

For example, excellent organizations:

- Use a key process framework to establish the organization strategy
- Manage their processes, from beginning to end, including those processes that exceed the bounds of the organization
- Ensure that the process owners understand what their role and responsibility is in the development, maintenance, and improvement of the processes
- Develop a significant set of performance indicators and results measures, enabling the revision of the efficiency and effectiveness of the core processes and their contribution to the strategic objectives

Criterion: Customer results

Definition

"Excellent organizations achieve and sustain outstanding results that meet or exceed the needs and expectations of their customers".

In practice, excellent organizations:

Use a set of measurements of perception and their performance indicators, based on the needs and expectations of their clients to determine the successful deployment of their strategy and support policies

- Establish clear objectives for the client-related core results, based on their needs and expectations, according to the selected strategy, segmenting the results to understand the experience, needs and expectations of the customer specific groups
- Showing positive or sustained clients-results for at least three years
- Understand clearly the reasons and key factors driving the observed trends and the effect that these results may have on other performance indicators, perceptions, and related results.
- Are confident in their performance and future results, and they rely on their understanding of the existing cause and effect relationships
- Interpret the comparison of the core results, which relate their clients with those of similar organizations and, where relevant, use these data to set objectives

Later we will describe the perception and performance indicators of the clients as internal measures to monitor and improve the process performance that created value for their clients.

We believe that these examples will make it clear to the reader that BPM is totally integrated in the EFQM excellence model. However, the EFQM model is non-prescriptive, and a best practice-based instrument that enables the organizations to have a generic structure of the corporate management system. From this perspective, the EFQM model is an excellent framework to introduce process-oriented Management (BPM); thus, it is totally integrated with quality management (TQM) in an organization.

4.2.3 RADAR Logic Scheme

The dynamic part of the EFQM management model is based on the "RADAR Logic Scheme". This is a management concept, and in turn, a dynamic scheme of assessment, whose foundations are in the well-known PDCA cycle (Planning, Developing, Monitoring, Acting). The RADAR cycle consists of four elements, as shown in figure 17:

- Required results
- Plan approaches
- Deploy approaches
- Assess and refine approaches

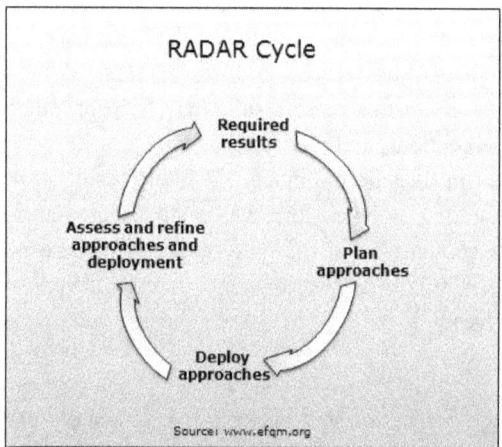

Figure 17 RADAR Cycle

The scheme describes the requirements of an organization to achieve the excellence:

Define the results to be achieved as part of the strategy process elaboration

- Planning and developing approaches properly based and integrated, which leads it to achieve the required results in the short, medium, and long-term

- Display the approaches systematically to ensure a successful implementation
- Assessing and reviewing the approaches used, based on processes of analysis of the results obtained, and incorporate continuous learning activities

RADAR for Enablers

In the version of the year 2013, it was developed a matrix to support the analysis of the five criteria approaches of the enablers (leadership, strategy, people, partnership & resources, processes). The description of the matrix has guidelines about what to expect the organization to demonstrate. Compared to the previous version of the year 2010, the general score should not exceed the partial approaches evaluated. For example, if the organization does not meet the requirements specified on some sub-criteria, the lowest valuation should be considered, as a whole. This change means, in practice, a stricter assessment than the preceding concepts. The criteria for assessing the approaches are the following:

- It cannot be proven: 0%
- Limited capacity to be proven: 25%
- It can be proven: 50%
- It can be fully proven: 75%
- It is recognized as a global reference model: 100%

Weighing with a RADAR tool

REDER is also used for scoring (evaluating) the reports of the organizations that apply to the EFQM Excellence Award, and to the European National Awards, but it can be used to conduct self-assessments as well, or to conduct benchmarking projects. The principle is given by the fact that the score goes up when the organization's performance improves. RADAR assigns a 50% to both, the facilitating agents and the results. Generally, within each criterion, the same specific weight is assigned to all the sub-criteria. Each sub-criterion is evaluated with the RADAR matrix, and the score is estimated. The base score covers 0 to 1.000 score-scale.

Finally, and in accordance with the EFQM model:

"The RADAR logic scheme provides a structured approach to analyze the performance of any organization. It is also the basis for the scoring system of the

EFQM Excellence Award, and to other initiatives of recognition or assessment, and may be useful to lead the change and manage improvement projects".

The strategic nature of the EFQM Model, combined with its focus on operational performance and a results orientation, makes it the ideal framework for testing the coherence and alignment of an organization's ambitions for the future, referenced against its current ways of working and its responses to challenges and pain-points. The EFQM Model structure is based on the simple but powerful logic of asking three questions (EFQM, 2019):

- "Why" does this organization exist? What Purpose does it fulfil? Why this particular strategy? (Direction)
- "How" does it intend to deliver on its Purpose and its Strategy? (Execution)
- "What" has it actually achieved to date? "What" does it intend to achieve tomorrow? (Results).

Central to the rationale of the EFQM Model, the "red thread", is the connection between the Purpose and Strategy of an organization and how that is used to help it Create Sustainable Value for its most important Stakeholders and deliver outstanding Results. The strategic nature of the EFQM Model, combined with its focus on operational performance and a results orientation, makes it the ideal framework for testing the coherence and alignment of an organization's ambitions for the future, referenced against its current ways of working and its responses to challenges and pain-points [39].

In November 2019, The EFQM launched the update of the new model, see figure 18, to co-create the new EFQM Model, nearly 2000 change experts were surveyed, facilitated 24 workshops internally, spoke face to face with leaders in over 60 diverse organizations and created a core team of experts and contributors from across industries and academia. From defining a strong purpose, inspiring leaders at every level and creating a culture committed to driving performance, while remaining agile, adaptive and able to evolve for the future, the new EFQM Model offers a framework that any organization can use to improve [40].

The EFQM Excellence Model 2020, this framework inclusive of seven main criteria:
1. Purpose, vision and strategy
2. Organizational culture and leadership
3. Engaging stakeholders
4. Creating sustainable value
5. Driving performance and transformation
6. Stakeholder perception
7. Strategic and operational performance

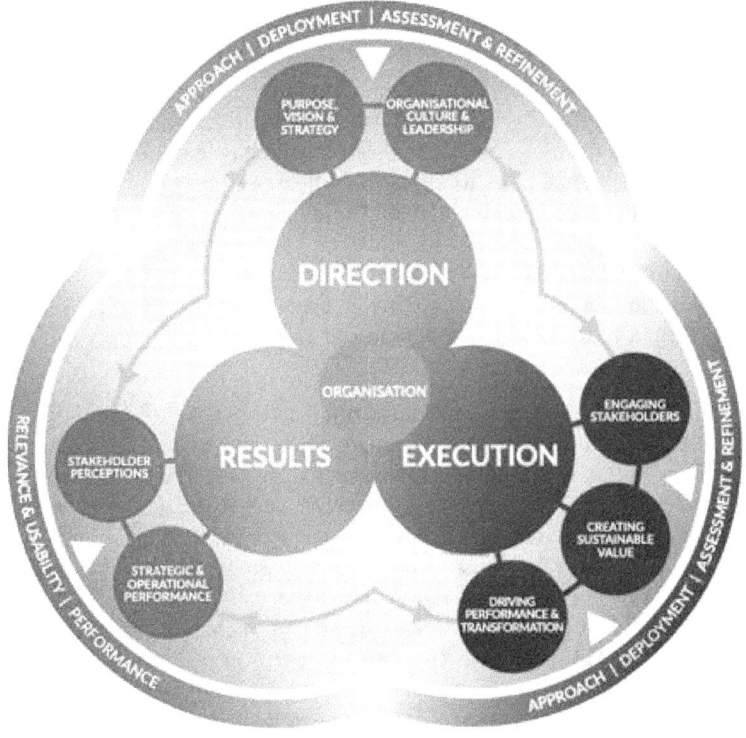

Figure 18 The EFQM Model 2020

4.3 Singapore Business Excellence Framework

The Singapore Business Excellence Framework is an initiative that was launched in 1994 by SPRING Singapore. The framework demonstrates how the drivers of performance influence the results achieved, in a cause-and-effect relationship. It is a roadmap for excellence that helps businesses understand how to improve performance. This is achieved through a thorough assessment of management processes based on the internationally benchmarked BE framework. The Singapore Business Excellence (BE) framework, which seeks to help enterprises strengthen fundamentals such as leadership, customer-centricity, people development, process capabilities, and knowledge management. They are conferred by the Singapore Quality Award (SQA) Governing Council and administered by SPRING Singapore. (Cham Tao Soon, chairman of the SQA Governing Council, 2013). Note: For all sources indicated here, see www.spring.gov.sg)

The Business Excellence (BE) initiative managed by SPRING Singapore provides organizations with a roadmap for excellence and helps them understand how they can improve their performance. This is done through a thorough assessment of their organizational performance based on the internationally benchmarked BE framework. With the dynamic business landscape and changing management trends, it is important for organizations to strengthen their business fundamentals to keep pace with economic developments and technological trends and seize new market opportunities. The existing four BE frameworks will be streamlined into one single framework. All organizations will pursue the Singapore Quality Class (SQC) as a required foundation before deepening niche capabilities of People, Service and Innovation. Organizations with outstanding performance can apply for the BE Awards (Spring Singapore, 2016).

The Singapore Business Excellence Framework provides a set of criteria, see figure 19 for organizational quality assessment and improvement and has been used by thousands of business, healthcare and educational organizations for more than 20 years. The criteria can be used as a tool for self-evaluation and are widely recognized as a robust framework for design and evaluation of any type of organizations. This framework also provides a comprehensive set of management standards for business excellence. It illustrates the cause and effect relationships between the drivers of performance and the results achieved. The Attributes of Excellence describe key characteristics of high performing organizations and are embedded throughout all the critical drivers of the framework. Besides the holistic BEF standard, there are three niches BE standards for people, innovation and service. As per their needs and strategies, organizations can choose any of the four BEF standards to enhance their capabilities.

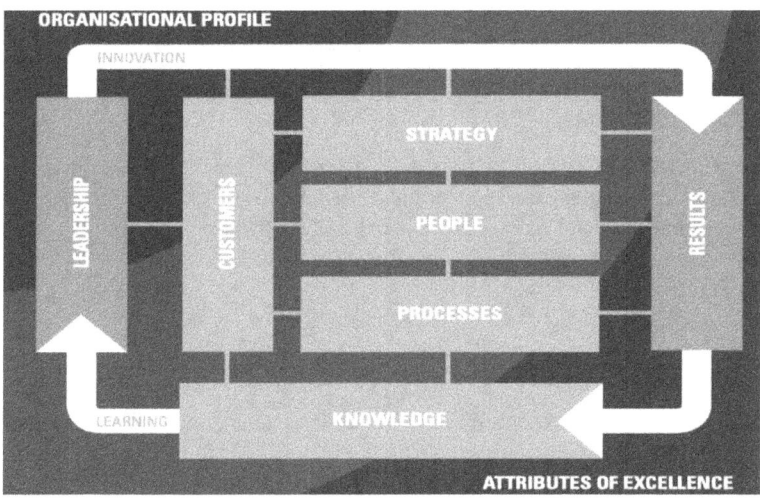

Figure 19: Singapore Business Excellence Framework

Singapore Business Excellence Initiative has a simple purpose: to provide the framework to help your organization, no matter its size or type (business, non-profit, education, government, healthcare) covering manufacturing, service, small businesses alike, focusing on knowing the critical aspects of managing and performing as an organization. It builds around an integrated performance management framework that the whole organization engages with, to improve overall performance and strive towards excellence (Spring Singapore, 2012).

Achieving & Sustaining Excellence in Public Services in Singapore

Today, citizens have access to a wide array of products and services delivered consistently with a high level of service from the private sector, and they expect a similar level of service from the government, so citizens have many expectations when it comes to government services. Many governments around the world such as the U.S., United Kingdom, United Arab Emirates, Singapore, and Canada have embarked on major reforms to enhance performance by adopting various strategies such as technology investment, developing alternate delivery channels, and implementing Business Excellence Frameworks. However, few governments have an established record of accomplishment or reputation for managerial excellence.

Singapore it's a clear example on how to be successfully adopting the Business Excellence Framework and accomplishment of great reputation in public sector. About two-thirds of public agencies in Singapore are BE-certified. A BE Interpretation Guide for the Public Sector was launched in 2013 to align the language of excellence to the key imperatives underpinning public sector transformation with a stronger focus on citizen-centricity, building trust and whole-of-government efforts. In 25 years, the Singapore Quality Award has recognized more than 2.000 organization, and many of these organization are from the public sector, like Singapore Police Force, National Library Board, Singapore Civil Defense Force, Housing & Development Board (HDB), Singapore Customs, among others.

"As Singapore progresses into the next phase of economic development, business excellence plays a greater role in helping organizations strengthen business fundamentals so that they can remain agile and seize growth opportunities," Source: Cham Tao Soon, chairman of the SQA Governing Council.

4.4 Dubai Business Excellence Framework-4G

In recent years, more and more governments entities have adopted performance excellence programs around the world. When successful, these programs unify a local or national's efforts to operate more efficiently, strengthen fiscal responsibility, and better serve citizens.

The Dubai Government Excellence Program (DGEP) is a pioneer program established with a clear vision, values and objectives in 1997 by His Highness Shaikh Mohammad Bin Rashid Al Maktoum the UAE Vice President, Prime Minister and Ruler of Dubai, aiming at engraving the culture of excellence in Dubai government and recognizing distinguished departments, teams and individuals [41].

The Business Excellence Framework was designed to enable the government entities of realizing the highest satisfaction rates and people's happiness and fulfil their needs and expectation regarding receipt of 7 stars' government services with the highest levels of efficacy and efficiency, as well as promotion of government trends in innovation field in order to provide a competitive advantage and reinforce the leading position of UAE.

The critical analysis carried out on the nine DGEP criteria, see figure 20, distributed into 38 main sub criteria and 200 sub-sub criteria found to be valid and reliable. The DGEP adopted the structure of the EFQM model and adapted to the UAE culture settings. Most of the DGEP model component linked strongly the five enablers "Leadership", "Strategy", "People", "Partnership" and "Resources and Process" with the model outcomes represented in the four types of results; people result, customer result, society result and key result.

"Excellence in development is an integral concept, inherent to the vertical and lateral building process for us in Dubai. In order to achieve excellence in the Arab world, all the elements of development, including its vision, goals, leadership and implementation, should be excellent" Source: H. H. Sheikh Mohammed Bin Rashid Al Maktoum, 2012, www.esma.gov.ae

Figure 20 Dubai Business Excellence Framework, 2020

Dubai Government New Challenges

Crown Prince of Dubai and Chairman of the Dubai Executive Council His Highness Sheikh Hamdan bin Mohammed bin Rashid Al Maktoum, said that the Dubai Government's Excellence Programs reflects the vision of Vice President and Prime Minister of the UAE and Ruler of Dubai His Highness Sheikh Mohammed bin Rashid Al Maktoum, which aims to continuously enhance government operations and processes to keep pace with changes and proactively deal with challenges so that Dubai will be a role model for future cities. Through the programs, Dubai seeks to enhance competitiveness and sustainability while also aligning itself with the government excellence system of the Ministry of Cabinet Affairs and the Future.

His Highness Sheikh Hamdan said that government operations require new models in order to match future requirements and ensure the highest standard of living for the people of Dubai. His Highness commended the role played by the Dubai Government Excellence Programs in encouraging government entities to maintain their efforts to achieve the highest levels of efficiency in government services. Dubai is among the world's best in terms of government efficiency and service levels.

The new initiatives of Dubai Government Excellence include (DGEP, 2020):

- An evaluation system that encourages government entities to develop and lead by competing on two levels: Basic level and Maturity level of excellence.
- An advanced evaluation system that includes new and variable axes for entities that achieve leadership positions among the maturity level of excellence "elite".
- A results-based evaluation system and measurement of the impact of government action.
- A system that enhances the transparency of the results of evaluation and clarifies the ranking of entities and how they compare with other entities.
- Advanced assessment reports that follow global best practices, as well as government-level excellence reports
- A mechanism for inter-agency cooperation and partnership to enhance their performance through knowledge and experience transfer.
- A new recognition framework that reflects leadership trends and priorities of the Dubai government.

Categories of Corporate Excellence for 2020:

- Elite Award
- Leading Government Award
- Best Entity for Innovation
- Best Achievement of Dubai Plan 2021
- The Happiest Working Environment
- The Best Entity in Digital Government
- Best Service Provider
- The Best Entity for Efficiency and Governance
- The Best Entity for Emiratization
- Most friendly environment for people of determination

"The Main objective is to maintain the high quality of life in Dubai, which requires innovative approaches. In Dubai, we create the future and don't wait for it.

Government excellence is also key to promoting corporate performance in Dubai, which further drives the sustainable development journey forward and promotes the efficient implementation of various strategic plans."

Source: H.H. Sheikh Hamdan bin Mohammed bin Rashid Al Maktoum, 2019

The excellence recipe that has been used by the UAE is also a unique blend, as it leads through disruption, and it emphasizes on generating accelerated momentums of delivery and performance impact. One could describe it as an approach to managing excellence through leading with agility to remain fresh and relevant but also to prevent complacency. Most governments in the world suffers from high levels of bureaucracy, obsolescence and old legacies that hamper progress and development in world that gradually requires speed and fast responsiveness [42].

5 ADOPTION OF A BPM BUSINESS EXCELLENCE FRAMEWORK

5.1 Business Excellence Framework and their integration with BPM

In the two preceding sections were presented two core concepts of BEF´s on the Baldrige and EFQM models. Most national and regional excellence models derive from these, so as an example here described Singapore and Dubai Business Excellence Framework. All this business excellence frameworks embrace the same principles, a holistic and systemic approach, process, and result. With the description and analysis of these frameworks, we can conclude that BPM is absolutely integrated with any of the Business Excellence Frameworks because it focuses on an approach for integrating the process criteria of the frameworks, for example if we use the Baldrige Criteria it integrated with the 6 processes criteria (what the organization does) with the core of Business Process Management, as we described in the chapter 1. These frameworks are "non-prescriptive", that is, they enable the organizations to have a generic structure to design their own "corporate process-oriented management system". However, it is important to follow the core principles and values over which these excellence models rest. Considering the above, both models (Baldrige and EFQM) provide an excellent reference framework to introduce "Process-oriented Management (BPM)" and integrate it with the "Business Excellence Frameworks (BEF)". This includes small or large organizations, private or public, be it for-profit or nonprofit.

BPM can be integrated through the definition of a BPM Governance model and relating it to each of the criteria (categories) of the selected BEF's. The Business Excellence frameworks and BPM are seamlessly integrated, almost naturally. BEF's models contribute to a structural reference framework, well defined and based on best practices to implement a corporate governance oriented to processes and results (integrated corporate management system). The BEF's also bring in metric definitions (quality standards) and provide a scoring system to assess the organizational performance in all the dimensions required by the stakeholder. BPM provides in turn, the necessary instruments to gather, document, analyze, design, implement, and measure the process results systematically, for each of the criteria of the BEF's models, in 3 categories:

1. Process cycle time (is the outcome process time for the customer acceptable?)
2. Process quality (is the compromised value delivered?)
3. Process cost (are we on budget by activity cost?)

As we know, BPM is connected to the central point of the triad: People - Production - Technology, and the excellence models are a reference framework, standardized, and provide a management method that seeks to achieve satisfaction of all the stakeholders through their People - Processes - Results.

Other criteria, as resources, and knowledge, can be abstracted in BPM as transversal categories, which, through their standardized processes are required for a good performance of the individuals. The BEF's also posit that the complete performance of an organization depends on the "Leadership" that conducts and drives the strategy, which is materialized through the "People", and, most important, its "Processes" implemented with IT systems, so we can take control by monitoring, where possible in real time. The leadership criterion belongs to the organizational development domain (soft skills). Although it is considered as a critical factor in BPM, it is not under the control of this discipline, but it does need to integrate its component; for example, through the knowledge management.

5.2 Example of Adoption of a BPM integrated BEF

As described before, the excellence models provide a well-defined structural reference framework, which is based on the best practices to implement a corporate governance, oriented to processes and results (integrated corporate management system). The excellence models contribute as well with the definition of metrics (quality standards) and provide a scoring system to assess the organizational performance in all the dimensions required by the stakeholders. In turn, BPM provides the necessary instruments to systematically evaluate, document, analyze, design, implement and measure the process results, for each of the criteria of the excellence models.

For instance, we will develop a generic governance model as a reference framework for Baldrige, but this exercise can also be developed for EFQM, Dubai, Singapore or other BEF's. The Baldrige model structure describes in its first block what the organizations does (the processes), and the second block, what the organization achieves (the results). This structure can be mapped to a BPM Governance model.

Figure 21 shows a proposal of integration of BPM Governance with the main categories of the Baldrige model.

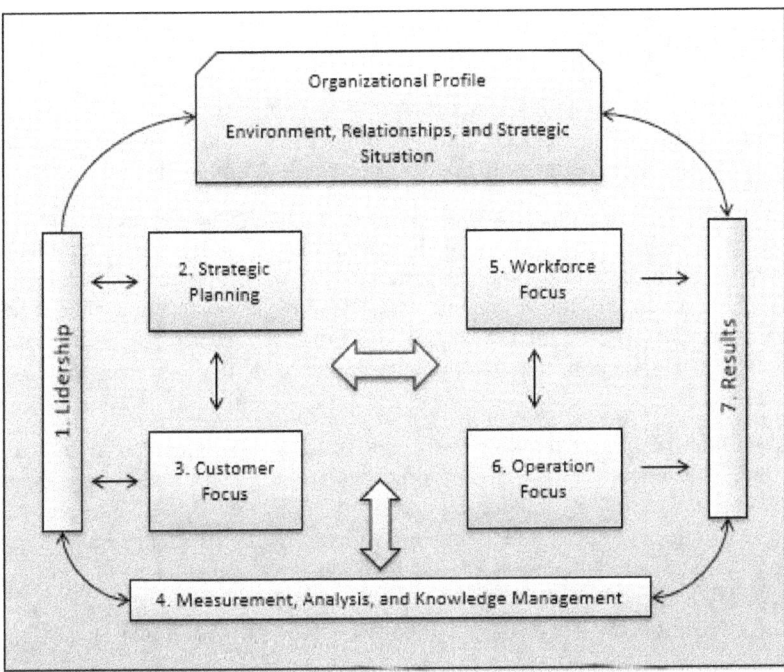

Figure 21 Example of a BPM Governance implementation for Baldrige Model

The BPM Governance cycle integrated with the Baldrige model begins with the occurrence of a new requirement, independent of its nature; for example, a change in the regulation: a new product or service is introduced, or a new strategy planning cycle starts. The impact of the requirement is analyzed in the strategic planning's (2.); in the Workforce processes (5.); in the business processes for operation (6.); and customer added value (3.). Through the facilitating agents, the change is planned, defined and implemented.

81

The process performance is monitored in operations (6.) in real time. The process results (7.) are measured for all stakeholders, and customer satisfaction. Then are analyzed, the results of the organizational performance, which are related to the degree of compliance of the business objectives (core results). All the deviations of the allowed ranges induce to a new learning, and to a proposal of improved change (4.).

The greatest contribution of BPM is that it interprets all the activities that a Business Excellence Framework defines and requires for its operation, to a process structure that can be managed and aligned with other organizational components for all sectors, including government agencies.

5.3 BPM Business Agility with DevOps

In BPM the term of business agility is understood as the ability of an organization to become adapted to the changing environment through changes in its own integrated processes. So, the faster the adaptation, the better business agility is obtained.

The term DevOps comes from software engineering to streamline development processes without lack of quality control. It is about establishing and assignment multidisciplinary business, development, operations and quality teams by managers (operations, plant, quality, IT, etc). The interesting features about this approach is to form a team around well-defined business functionality. These teams become accountable for management of this functionality and they are the only ones to make the requested changes.

DevOps is evolutionary in its thinking with regards how IT services are delivered and supported. The schools of thought and practices are largely based on preceding work in the area of Continuous Integration and Application Life Cycle Management (ALM) and is therefore rooted in the agile philosophy, which also attempts to bridge the traditional organizational process divide between development and operations teams. DevOps is a combination of the words "Development" (Dev) and "Operations" (Ops). It is not a mythology, or software, but a way of doing [43].

Figure 22 shows that the DevOps team is formed at the intersection of the development, QA and operations views.

Figure 22 forming a unit DevOps

A recent IASA article [43] describes very well how the administration of this new unit works.

"DevOps practices include the use of existing disciplines, e.g. governance, quality assurance (QA), testing, security and release management, but extends this work-effort to include disciplines involving people, culture, processes, tools and methodologies that reduce risk and cost, enables technology to change at the speed of the business, and improve overall quality. This aims to solve a fundamental business problem: reduce the time to-market for new products and features based on ever evolving customer needs; quickly resolve operational and support issues and; show greater responsiveness to changing (internal and external) environmental situations."

Figure 23 DevOps framework – Based on work performed by Intel

"The framework of figure 23 depicts the DevOps process design, systems and tools development and deployment, and social and organizational issues. The outcomes of

83

DevOps are Continuous Integration (CI) and Continuous Deployment (CD) of product functionality and infrastructure setup. These characteristics are not unique to DevOps, and indeed, are generally applicable to enterprises with respect to enterprise agility and enterprise digital transformation." [43]

This concept is aligned with all the layers of organizations in charge of managing change and applying agile methodologies to achieve greater business agility. BPM offers this approach to its change management cycle to achieve greater business agility in executing the weighted project plans of the Business Excellence initiative.

To understand this in the context of our BPM integration, as tools to support the initiatives of a Business Excellence project, we are going to remind the reader that Business Excellence Frameworks are "non-prescriptive", that is, they leave the organization free on how to implement your improvement initiatives.

Also exists another problem, after raising the opportunities for improvement of the BEF criteria to be used for weighing, which will be implement first and which later. The framework does not offer these criteria, nor does it want to enter these methodological discussions. Different is in BPM.

BPM as a management discipline is not "prescriptive", but it does require defining a governance model to align the objectives with Strategic Planning. We recommend deducing the strategic objectives from the business model, which defines the value proposition for the client. That is the mission that must be accomplished and from there the objectives can be deduced, for example from a canvas model. For each of the segments, key factors can be defined as guiding objectives for achieving the value proposition. These objectives can support the weighting of BEF's diagnostic improvement initiatives.

So, how do we form these DevOps teams according to BPM process-oriented management. The processes are identified first (see process architecture). For each business process, the stages that cover different "business functionalities" are identified, then the groups of these business functionalities are assigned to teams DevOPs. Also, these teams are then responsible for implementing the improvement initiatives selected on a BEF roadmap.

Figure 24 schematically shows how this improvement cycle of integration between BPM and BEF works

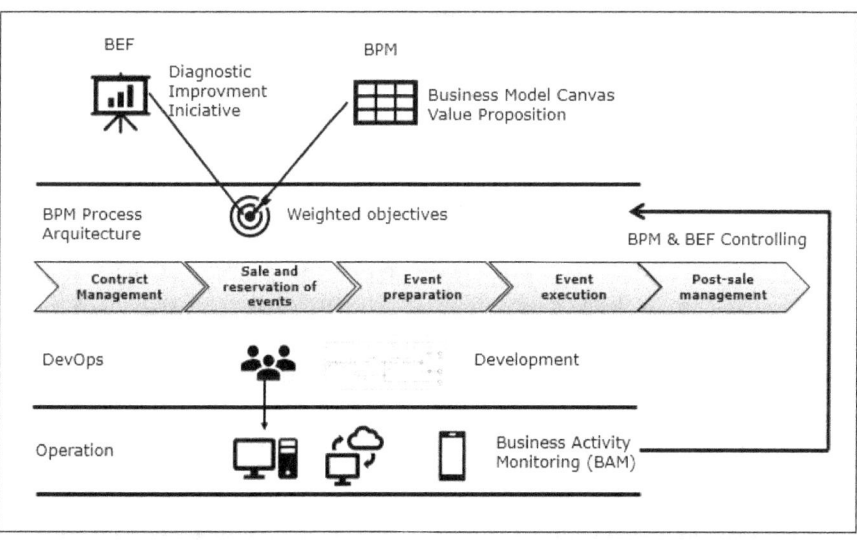

Figure 24 DevOPs integration concept to achieve greater business agility

Source: own elaboration

6 BENCHMARKING

6.1 Introduction

Knowledge on best practices provides a competitive advantage for organizations in the knowledge-based economy. Whether in manufacturing or services, in the private or public sector, enterprises must benchmark themselves against the best standards or practices worldwide to achieve a competitive advantage and business excellence. Benchmarking is all about making comparisons, and comparability requires consistent definitions—apples must be compared to apples. Comparability also requires a consistent methodology, including how data are defined, collected, cleansed, validated, analyzed, and summarized into performance metrics.

Robert Camp (1989) [44] defines benchmarking as "the continuous process of measuring products, services and practices against the toughest competitors or those companies recognized as industry leaders, (that is) ... the search for industry best practices that will lead to superior performance". 'Given the fact that industry best practice for a given product, service or process may never be found, because of high transactions costs, only relative or local optimums are found as benchmarks. In the real world "ideal type" definitions of benchmarking need, however, to be modified. Consequently, benchmarking is a continuous, systematic process of measuring products, services and practices against organizations regarded to be superior with the aim of rectifying any performance "gaps"'.

Benchmarking is a change management approach that sparks and enables innovation. Benchmarking provides solutions and not just comparisons. Benchmarking through "learning from the experience of others' and seeing new and different approaches changes mindsets and opens up new possibilities – this leads to paradigm shifts and innovation. Benchmarking includes the process of identifying, adapting, creating, and implementing high performing practices to produce superior performance results.

Benchmarking involves comparing a current data set to historical data sets or data from industry peers. It can help consultants determine where clients are ahead of competition, identify areas for client improvement, boost the quality of the firm's IP, and increase the firm's competitive value. Benchmarking is frequently used to aid strategic and business planning, as part of an ongoing performance management program, to support significant initiatives

Organizations, like people, are organisms that are subject to universal truths. In this step, I will share with you the modern quality tool called "benchmarking." This is the practice of observing, analyzing and learning from your peers and competitors. It's likely that there are organizations out there that are already doing it right, organizations that are more competitive and that have established a healthy, ethical working environment.

Benchmarking is a modern quality tool. It is widely used across developed countries as a formal methodology. It is also informally utilized in lesser-developed countries. For example, when two airlines determine their ticket prices based on observing each other's business behavior (Doctor Camp calls this "competition benchmarking"). Benchmarking began to spread across the world in the early '90s and proliferated within service businesses, manufacturing, healthcare, government, and educational organizations. Benchmarking is a means of measurement. It's a process of analyzing your organization's products, services, and processes and comparing them to those of other successful organizations. When you benchmark you look for companies that have mastered aspects of their business in any sector. To be successful, benchmarking should be implemented as a structured, systematic process. It will not be successful if applied in an ad hoc fashion on a random basis. Ultimately, benchmarking is about being humble enough to admit that others are better at something and being wise enough to learn how match—or even surpass—them at it.

Informal Benchmarking

This is a type of benchmarking that most of us do unconsciously at work and in our home life. We constantly compare and learn from the behavior and practices of others—whether it is how to use a software program, cook a better meal, or play our favorite sport. In the context of work, most learning from informal benchmarking comes from the following:

- Talking to colleagues and learning from their experience (coffee breaks and team meetings are a great place to network and learn from others)
- Consulting with experts (for example, business consultants who have experience of implementing a particular process or activity in many business environments);
- Networking with people from other organizations at conferences, seminars, and internet forums
- Websites, online databases, and publications that share benchmarking information provide quick and easy ways to learn of best practices and benchmarks.

Formal benchmarking consists of two types – performance benchmarking and best practice benchmarking:

a) **Performance benchmarking** describes the comparison of performance data obtained from studying similar processes or activities. Performance benchmarking may involve the comparison of financial measures (such as expenditure, cost of labour, and cost of buildings/equipment) or non-financial measures (such as absenteeism, staff turnover, complaints, and call center performance).

b) **Best practice benchmarking** describes the comparison of performance data obtained from studying similar processes or activities and identifying, adapting, and implementing the practices that produced the best performance results. The Xerox methodology can be described as a best practice benchmarking methodology.

It is important to distinguish between performance benchmarking and best practice (or process) benchmarking.

Performance benchmarking refers to the comparison of process output as a means of identifying opportunities for improvement, setting performance targets, and understanding relative positioning in comparison to other organizations.

Best practice benchmarking refers to the comparison of the actual processes, practices and procedures (as opposed to just performance levels) in order to gain detailed knowledge of how improvements can be made. Most organizations use performance benchmarking (comparing of performance) rather than the more powerful but resource intensive approach of benchmarking for best practices (comparing and learning from others and implementing best practices). Performance Benchmarking [45]

Benchmarking is a core component of continuous improvement programs. As Gregory Watson noted in his Benchmarking Workbook, 12 of the 32 criteria for the Malcolm Baldrige National Quality Award refer to benchmarking as a key component of quality assurance and process improvement.

Benchmarking requires an understanding of what is important to the organization (sometimes called critical success factors) and then measuring performance for these factors. The gap between actual performance and preferred achievement is typically analyzed to identify opportunities for improvement.

Benchmarking brings an external focus on internal activities, functions, or operations in order to achieve continuous improvement. Starting from an analysis of existing activities and practices within the firm, the objective is to understand existing processes or activities and then to identify an external point of reference or standard by which that activity can be measured or judged.

Performance Benchmarking it is concerned with comparing your company's products and services. This tool focuses on product and service quality, features, price, speed, reliability, design and customer satisfaction. In addition, you can benchmark anything that has measurable metrics, including processes. Performance benchmarking is usually the first step organizations take to identify performance gaps.

Most people equate benchmarking to performance benchmarking. This is unfortunate, because performance benchmarking on its own is of limited use. Too often performance benchmarking data are collected (often at significant cost) and no further action is taken after the data have been obtained. While performance benchmarking enables a performance gap to be identified, it does not provide the idea, best practice, or solution as to how performance can be improved and the gap closed [46].

Types of Benchmarking (Camp R., 1989)

Research studies have suggested that there are four commonly accepted approaches to (or 'types' of) best practice benchmarking. These are as follows:

1. **Internal benchmark**

In large organizations, which operate in different geographic locations or manage many products and services, same functions and processes are usually performed by different teams, business units or divisions. This often results in processes performed very well in one division but poorly in another. For Examples Banks, Retails, Energy & Oil Companies.

Internal benchmarking compares separate teams, units or divisions internal to an organization. This exercise identifies the entities that are work better and share the knowledge with other teams to achieve higher performance. Usually, companies benchmark internal units to create channels to diffuse best practices, promote knowledge sharing, and improve communications. One example is Boeing company in US. They used Malcolm Baldrige Quality Framework in all their manufacturing plants in order to improve the performance.

2. **Competitive benchmark**

It's the comparison and identification of performance gaps in relation to an organization's direct competitors. As a process, competitive benchmarking on its own may be limiting, since it is difficult to obtain useful and accurate information from competitors. For example: same industry: Oil & Energy Business, Retails, Banks, Government agencies, etc. External benchmarking looks both, inside and outside the industry to find the best practices. Organizations have developed different ways to overcome this challenge of accessing data and facilitating competitive benchmarking. These include 'blind' comparisons, using intermediaries and benchmarking areas of mutual concern that are likely to be less competitively sensitive (e.g., the areas of health and safety, the prevention of money laundering and the reduction of insurance fraud). It's important to highlight that Competitive benchmarking, often used with performance benchmarking, compares products and services, NO strategy, because it'll be very hard to find a competitor that is willing to share sensitive information.

3. **Generic benchmark**

Generic benchmark focus on excellent work processes rather than on the business practices of a organization. This refers to comparisons with non-competing organizations that are known to have best practices in specific functions. The organization to be benchmarked may or may not be in the same industry but the functions to be compared need to have some similarity. For example, your company tries to improve its marketing capabilities and benchmarks itself against a competitor. While observing the competitor's marketing processes, you notice how well their human resources are managed using data analytics. Also, in the airlines industry when 2 companies compare prices or destinations.

4. **Strategic benchmark**

Strategic Benchmarking refers to the comparison of long-term strategies and general approaches that have enabled high performers to succeed. It involves considering high-level aspects such as core competencies, the development of new products and services, and improving capacity for dealing with changes in the external environment. This type of benchmarking is useful for realigning business strategies that have become inappropriate.

6.2 Benchmarking for Best Practices

Best practices are those practices that have been shown to produce superior results; selected by a systematic process; and judged as exemplary, good, or successfully demonstrated [47].

"There is no single "best practice" because best is not best for everyone. Every organization is different in some way–different missions, cultures, environments, and technologies. What is meant by "best" are those practices that have been shown to produce superior results; selected by a systematic process; and judged as exemplary, good, or successfully demonstrated. Best practices are then adapted to fit a particular organization." (Dr. Robert Camp, 2012 Honorary Life-time President, Global Benchmarking Network)

Benchmarking for best practices provides a good learning opportunity for those involved in the process, in addition to stimulating their creativity and stretching their cognitive ability. The possibilities of bringing about useful changes in the organization and the benefits of such change also become evident. 'Seeing is believing' as the saying goes, seeing the viability of certain ideas, processes and activities and their successful implementation by other companies, tends to bolster one's self-confidence and the belief that what other can do, one can do even better. However, it's true that we need to be humble. Understanding our value, and acknowledging that we are good, should not prevent us from knowing that there's always new to learn. We can´t never stop learning, because benchmarking it´s a journey not a destination.

The name of TRADE reminds users to develop strong two-way relationships with other organizations in order to share or trade information and best practices for mutual benefit. TRADE was initially developed for the New Zealand Benchmarking Club which existed between 2000 and 2004. In 2007, the methodology was significantly enhanced when COER was commissioned to provide the benchmarking methodology for Singapore's public sector. In 2009, further developments to the methodology were made with the introduction of a certification scheme to increase the professionalism of benchmarking. Today, in 2019, TRADE, see figure 25 is continuing to grow in use with, for example, it becoming the methodology of choice for Dubai's Government Excellence Programs as part of its drive to encourage innovation in the public sector.

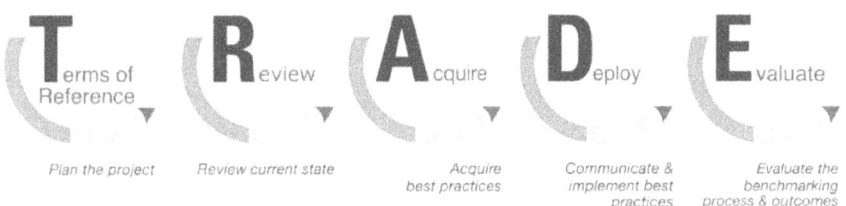

Figure 25 TRADE methodology, Dr. Robin Mann

Measuring performance against a recognized business excellence or quality framework can deliver a range of benefits for any organization. It is pivotal to a firm to know one's own standard and compare it against others in today's complex and competitive corporate environment.

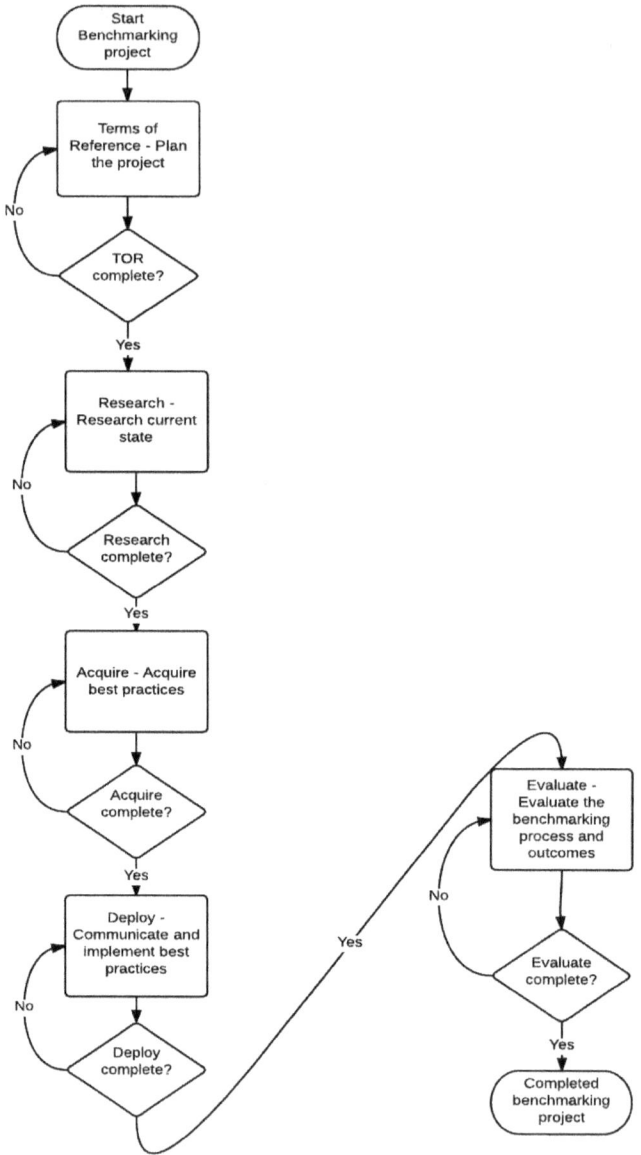

Figure 26 TRADE benchmarking process described using a process flow chart

A best practice is a method or technique that has been generally accepted as superior to any alternatives because it produces results that are superior to those achieved by other means or because it has become a standard way of doing things, e.g., a standard way of complying with legal or ethical requirements.

Also, a best practice is an industry-wide agreement that standardizes the most efficient and effective way to accomplish a desired outcome. A best practice generally consists of a technique, method, or process. The concept implies that if an organization follows best practices, a delivered outcome with minimal problems or complications will be ensured. Best practices are often used for benchmarking and represent an outcome of repeated and contextual user actions.

The BPIR Improvement Cycle

The BPIR cycle is an adaptation of Codling's [48] 12-stage benchmarking process. In the initial design stages, the 12-stage benchmarking process was used to identify potential information that could be used to assist the benchmarking process. Figure 27 was then adapted after feedback from BPIR users and consideration of the type of improvement information that had been collected.

The BPIR improvement cycle also facilitates the process of benchmarking best practice. This 9-step cycle has some core similarities with the Camp and Mann's methodologies. The BPIR cycle consists of the following:

1. Identify/select an area for improvement;
2. Measure performance;
3. Benchmark performance;
4. Identify a relevant improvement approach or strategy;
5. Learn how to implement;
6. Identify best practice organizations;
7. Research further information;
8. Implement a best practice approach;
9. Review and calibrate.

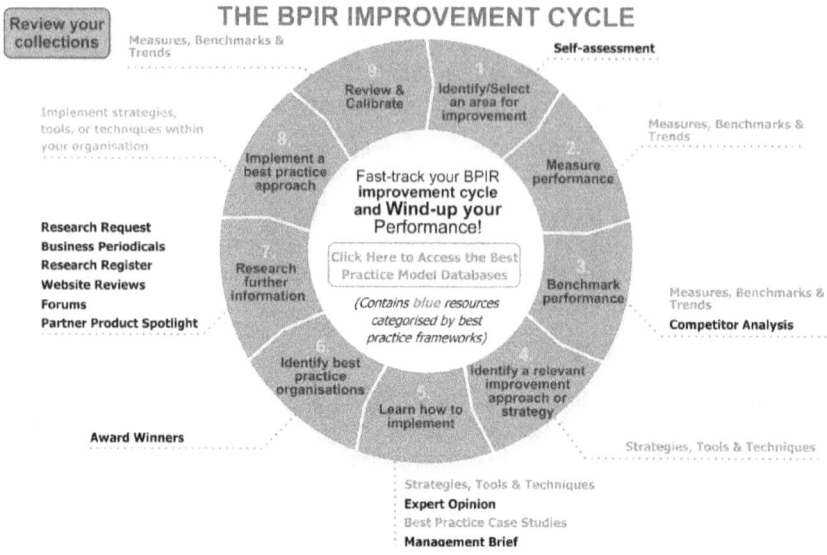

Figure 27 BPIR's improvement cycle showing key services/information types available to support each activity in the cycle

A key advantage of the BPIR framework is the availability of extensive on-line resources to guide the practitioner through each of the stages. These resources are of value to both experienced and novice benchmarking practitioners and help to reduce the time it takes to undertake a benchmarking project.

Main benefits of Benchmarking

In our experience, working with different organizations around the world, benchmarking has many different benefits (tangibles and intangibles), but we think the most important are related with the intangibles benefits for example, building a culture of continuous improvement and established a solid foundation in the entire organization. To fully evaluate the impact of benchmarking, it is necessary to undertake, where possible, a quantitative assessment of impact with calculable values assigned. Professors Dr. Mohammed Zairi summarized the operational and cultural benefits of benchmarking in the following way:

- Removes the need to 'reinvent the wheel';
- Leads to 'outside-the-box' thinking, encouraging organizations to look for ways to improve that come from outside;
- Forces organizations to examine current processes, which can often lead to improvement in itself;

- Accelerates change and restructuring by using tested and proven methods and creating a sense of urgency when gaps are identified;
- Allows the organization to focus externally and constantly capture opportunities and counter potential threats;
- Helps prevent complacency and inertia within the organization and its people by setting stretch goals and stimulating new ways to plan for the future;
- Promotes the emergence and evolution of a 'learning culture' throughout the organization;
- Promotes the development of a customer-centric culture by constantly reminding people of the customer and focusing on critical processes that add value;
- Overcomes the 'not-invented-here' mindset by offering evidence that ideas invented outside the organization can and do work.

6.3 Dubai: We Learn Initiative

The "Dubai We Learn" initiative was launched in October 2015 as part of the Dubai Government Excellence Program (DGEP) knowledge sharing initiatives. The DGEP is a program of the General Secretariat of the Executive Council of Dubai. The "Dubai We Learn" initiative was launched in cooperation with the Centre of Organizational Excellence Research (COER) from New Zealand. From DGEP's perspective benchmarking is considered a powerful tool for organizational learning and knowledge sharing. This kind of initiatives that Dubai Government Excellence Program launched 3 years ago, enhance Dubai's image as an international hub in the area of government administration, quality, knowledge sharing, excellence, creativity and organizational learning.

In 2019, Dubai We Learn completed its 3rd Cycle, the Final (4th) Knowledge Sharing Summit of the Dubai Government Excellence Program (DGEP) with the participation of 11 governments projects, like:

- Dubai Police: Airport Secure Luggage (Safe Bags);
- Dubai Municipality: Digital Transformation of contracts;
- Dubai Health Authority (DHA): Dubai Heart Safe City Initiative.

On December 22th, the final event attended by project sponsors, key stakeholders, guests and project team members, the projects were scrutinized for their quality and evaluated for their performance impact by an esteemed expert panel of judges. The 7 Star projects (based on the Best Practice Certification System) that received a TRADE Benchmarking Proficiency Certificate with Commendation were:

- Dubai Municipality: Digital Transformation of Contracts
- Dubai Police: Airport Secure Luggage (Safe Bags)
- Dubai Corporation for Ambulance Services: Moonshot: Is Where Magic Happens

Assessment grades	Certificate Awarded	Explanation
7 Stars	TRADE Benchmarking Proficiency Certificate with Commendation	Role Model, World-Class, Wow!
5-6 Stars	TRADE Benchmarking Proficiency Certificate with Commendation	Excellence, Outstanding, Exceeds Expectations
3-4 Stars	TRADE Benchmarking Proficiency Certificate	Competent, Professional
1-2 Stars	Incomplete	Incomplete

Figure 28 TRADE Best Practice Certification System, 2018

6.4 Dubai Police Case Study: Call of Duty (TRADE Methodology)

6.4.1 *An overview of the Dubai Police*

The organization in this case study it is the Dubai Police (DP). Since Dubai Police was founded in 1956, a great attention has been paid to social responsibility with its various dimensions. Dubai Police aims to provide quality services to all segments of society to win their satisfaction and exceed their expectations, Dubai Police use Business Excellence Framework (EFQM, Baldrige and Dubai Government Excellence Program) and formal Benchmarking (TRADE Methodology) to assets their performance in order to offers an outstanding service to the stakeholders. Dubai Police's services are not only limited to maintain security and stability but exceed to cover the requirements of the society. The Strategic Plan contains objectives that meet the expectations and aspirations of its customers and guarantees their satisfaction, which stems from the strategic plan of the Government of the Emirate of Dubai. DP has always strived to maintain the highest levels of comfort, security and safe living for its visitors and residents. The fact that 97.8% of the people feel it is safe and secure to walk out at night in the UAE, has ranked the country as the top of world's safest place. UAE's policies and strategies were behind the achievements to make the country one of the safest countries in the world. (Gallup, 2018).

Since 2014, Dubai Police are applying a formal methodology of Benchmarking "TRADE" (Dr. Robin Mann) and this methodology is using among different department and projects which allows Dubai Police to always research for the best practices, among police forces and others sectors as well, and also to create a sustainable knowledge management. Here we described how the TRADE methodology can be applied to all of the Dubai Police Departments. In this case study, The Mechanical Department of Transport and Rescue developed a project called: "Call of Duty", a 7 starts project from Dubai We Learn 2018. In 2019, the Airport Department is part of the Dubai We Learn Program with the project called "Safe Bag".

6.4.2 Call of duty

The Mechanical Department of Transport and Rescue is one of the keys enabling and operational departments of Dubai Police. It is a technical department that focuses on the maintenance and repair of vehicles to ensure their optimum use. The Mechanical Department can service almost every make of car manufactured in the world, as well as marine and rescue vehicles – this is no easy feat, especially if you consider our unique fleet of high-performance vehicles, which includes a Lamborghini, BMW, Maserati, Audi, Ferrari and a Bentley

The department has 7 main sections with more than 150 employees that fulfil the following objectives:

1. Maintenance and repair of Dubai Police vehicles.
2. Development of specifications and mechanisms based on special requests from general departments, administrations, and police stations
3. Preparation of technical reports to demonstrate the availability of vehicles and to determine future utilization.
4. Preparation of technical reports as testimony or evidence for courts and police stations in the cases of traffic/mechanical accidents.

The underlying drivers for this benchmarking project were manifold. They included the need to provide standardized, regulated working hours for each maintenance and repair task and to achieve uniformity in employee labour hours. It was also important to develop appropriate metrics for productivity, efficiency, and effectiveness while understanding obstacles and issues affecting technician productivity. The benchmarking project would also contribute to implementing institutional identity and strategic objectives of Dubai Police and achieve the objectives of the National Agenda "Dubai Vision 2021".

- Project Aim (Term of References)

The aim of the project was to find and implement best practices in vehicle fleet maintenance to improve vehicle availability and labour productivity of the Dubai Police Mechanical Department to world class levels. The specific targets set were to increase productivity for the Mechanical Department from 40% to 70%, and consequently, increase vehicle availability from 88% to 95%. The focus of these targets were police patrol vehicles which account for approximately 800 vehicles of the total fleet of approximately 3,600 vehicles. At the level of individual employees in the Mechanical Department, this project aimed to increase the productive hours of each technician from 2.4 hours per day to 6 hours per day and reduce the average repair time per task by a minimum of 5%.

- Research Stage

During the research phase, the team conducted an extensive review of factors that were impeding labor productivity and vehicle availability. This involved SWOT analysis, fishbone analysis, surveying the opinions of mechanics, analyzing job sheet data, and deciding on the most important performance measures to use. The main areas of concern were identified in the fishbone diagram:

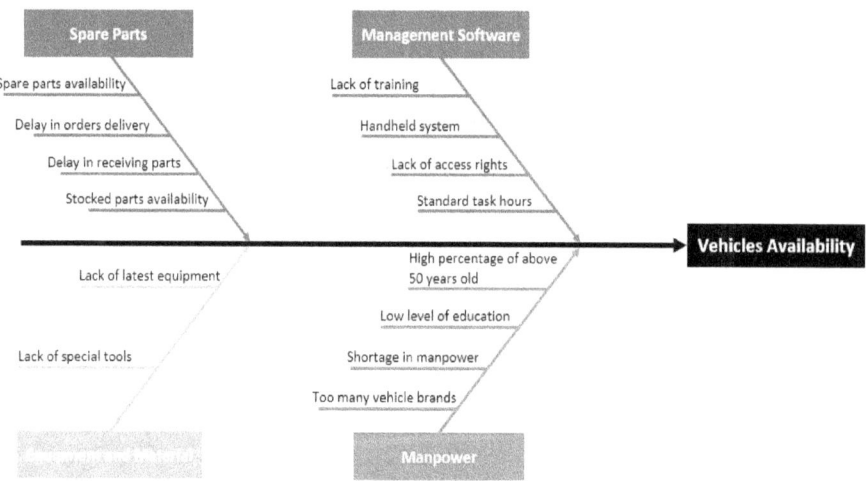

Figure 29 Fishbone diagram of vehicle availability

- Acquire Stage

At the beginning of the Acquire stage, Dubai Police defined 12 criteria for the selection of potential benchmarking partners. The potential benchmarking partners were divided as follows:

1) Core Benchmarking Partners: these partners were organizations or businesses with the same core functions and activities as Dubai Police
2) Creative Benchmarking Partners: these partners were organizations or businesses with different core functions and activities.

Potential Benchmarking partners were then approached and ultimately, nine organizations were visited for the purposes of benchmarking exchange. This number and variety of benchmarking partners enabled the collection of significant depth and breadth of high-quality information. For example, at Avis, the benchmarking team gained detailed knowledge of the management of staff time and happiness, the mechanisms used to achieve high level performance results and managing the supply chain of spare parts. At the end of this stage, 23 ideas/best practices were recommended for implementation.

- Deploy Stage

The deploy stage began with the benchmarking team developing an initial action plan for the best practices selected. This was then shared in a presentation to the General Director of Transport & Rescue as well as managers and technicians of the Mechanical Works Department. Meetings with these stakeholders resulted in further refinement of the action plans and gave all stakeholders a sense of ownership of the actions with the managers and certain technicians becoming a supporting team for the project.

- Evaluate Stage

The results showed an increase in labor productivity from 40% to 72.2% and an increase in vehicle availability from 88% to 95% saving US$ 4 million. If performance levels are maintained this will result in an annual recurring saving of more than US$ 2.2 million per year with savings in excess of US$ 5.5 million in the first year. Dubai Police were awarded TRADE Benchmarking Proficiency Certificate with Commendation (7 Stars) by the Centre for Organizational Excellence Research and Dubai We Learn 2018.

Some of the main the Benefits:

Non-financial benefits achieved within one year and expected future benefits:

- Increase in labor productivity from 40% to 72% and vehicle availability from 88% to 95%
- Increase in average actual hours working on job tasks of each mechanic from 2.4 hours per day to 5 hours per day.
- Reduced average repair time per task by at least 5% Standardized working hours encouraged employees to accomplish tasks promptly and enabled management to identify performance issues quickly.

Financial benefits achieved within one year and expected future benefits:

- Savings of US$ 1.5 million (Aug-2017 to Mar-2018) due to a decrease in downtime cost of patrol vehicles.
- Saving of US$ 2.4 million due to increased vehicle availability of 5%, eliminating replacement costs of 40 vehicles.
- Closing down all operations of the mini workshop saves US$ 71.000 per year.

Conclusion and new challenges

Dubai Police had not only maintained its performance levels, they had sought new ways to improve the maintenance of their fleet vehicles. In particular, they had streamlined the delivery of parts and particularly high value parts. This had been achieved by working in partnership with parts suppliers and it meant that stock was now better managed to meet high demands and short lead-times. Perhaps the most important outcome of Dubai Police's involvement in the "Dubai We Learn" initiative is the acceptance and widespread deployment of benchmarking and improvement activities based on the TRADE methodology. All departments and sections of Dubai Police are now set KPIs linked to benchmarking improvement. The performance of the departments and sections of Dubai Police against the KPIs set are monitored on an annual basis and there is a General Commander Award for the best performers. The commitment of Dubai Police to continual improvement and the use of benchmarking as an improvement tool has led to significant external recognition of their performance and achievement. Continuous improvement it's part of DP's DNA and Dubai Police will keep working with Benchmarking for Best Practices in order to performance better and be in a leading position around the world.

6.5 Business Process Management integrated with Benchmarking

Through the Business Process Management System (BPMS), business processes are being modeled, monitored, simulated (reevaluating their performance indicators and their benchmark) in order to be constantly improved. As we explained in the chapter 6, how benchmarking can be used by organizations to help them increase their productivity and improve their business processes. Benchmarking for best practices performs all the potential data for performance measurement in order to add value to your organization and not to invent the wheel. BPM provides the necessary instruments to systematically evaluate, document, analyze, design, implement and measure the process results, for each of the criteria of the excellence models.

The Business Excellence Frameworks' structure describes in its first block what the organizations does (the processes), and the second block, what the organization achieves (the results). This structure can be mapped to a BPM Governance model supported by Benchmarking for Best Practices (TRADE methodology). Also in the chapter 5, we gave an example of adoption of a BPM integrated with the Malcolm Baldrige Framework, as you know all of the BEF's around the world have many things in commons, and it's the continuous learning from the best that will help the organization to performance better

6.6 Summary

The Business Excellence Frameworks provide a holistic approach to continuous improvement for any type of organization. These frameworks that we just mentioned in this chapter are based on concepts and principles and have proved their viability during the time. Consequently, they gave birth to frameworks that allow organizations to benchmark their performances and demonstrate best practices in their field of activity, also we described a formal methodology "TRADE" of Benchmarking from Dr. Robin Mann and how all types of organization can benefit of using this type of Benchmarking. We explained the initiative of DGEP with Dubai We Learn and how some organization in the public sector improved the performance applying projects to TRADE.

In the beginning, the business excellence frameworks were adapted to the needs of big businesses (mainly manufacturing companies), but in time, new attempts have been made in order to create and develop these models for small and medium enterprises and for different types of organization like non-profit, government, education and business (profit). American Society for Quality (ASQ) mentioned back in 2015, that in US majority of the organization using the Baldrige criteria are in the Healthcare sector.

The Business Excellence Frameworks allows organizations to understand and build management fundamentals and guide them towards achieving higher performance. To benefit from the initiative, organizations should continuously refer the BEF to review their internal systems and processes and to systematically challenge the companies to achieve better results. As the business landscape evolves, EFQM, Baldrige, Singapore, Dubai frameworks regularly updates the Business Excellence initiative to ensure its continued relevance and robustness. Excellent organizations have a positive impact on the world around them by enhancing their performance whilst simultaneously advancing the economic, environmental and social conditions within the communities they touch.

One of the challenges facing excellence awards programs globally is ensuring that these programs add value and remain just as relevant to SMEs, NGO, as to large organizations including multinationals and government agencies.

Given today's uncertain global economic environment, it is crucial for all agencies around the world that manage the business excellence frameworks to strengthen their business fundamentals to be able to take on any challenges that come their way and maintain long-term business viability, as we mentioned the best practices frameworks like Dubai and Singapore, they also need to be update and keep adding value to all the government agencies.

Economic environment is being reshaped by new industry (industrial revolution 4.0), digital transformation and technology trends, which are disrupting business models and fundamentally changing jobs around the world. In this regard, we truly believe that Business Excellence Framework will continue to be a key enabler for organizations looking to gain a competitive edge, increase productivity, engage the stakeholders and transform themselves for the future.

7 APPENDIX

7.1 Acknowledgement to the Reader

We would like to thank the reader for having caught his interest, and for placing his trust in this work, taking the time in reading and studying it. We hope this book will help everyone to become initiated or gain new knowledge the world of BPM, BEF and Benchmarking.

If you work on the improvement of the process management in your organization by implementing BPM, you will be automatically contributing to the best value creation of the company, to their clients. Then, the goal of this book has been accomplished as well.

We would like to further improve this work in the coming issues; therefore, we would appreciate your sending your feedback to jroman@businessexcellence.cl and, bernhard.hitpass@usm.cl.

7.2 Glossary

API	Application Programming Interface
BAM	Business Activity Monitoring
BEF	Business Excellence Framework
BPA	Business Process Analysis
BPM	Business Process Management
BPMN	Business Process Model and Notation
BPMS	BPM Suite or System
BRMS	Business Rules Management Systems
CPS	Cyber Physical System
DevOps	Development and Operation Unit
EA	Enterprise Architecture
ESB	Enterprise Service Bus
IoE	Internet of Everything
IoT	Internet of Thinks
MBNQA	Malcolm Baldrige National Quality Award
OCR	Optical Character Recognition
OT	Operational Technologies
QA	Quality Assurance
SOA	Service Oriented Architecture
TQM	Total Quality Management

7.3 List of Figures

Figure 1: BPM Process-based cycle 12
Figure 2 Structuring levels of the process architecture 14
Figure 3 Representation of value chain type configuration 15
Figure 4 Representation of value shop type configuration 16
Figure 5 Representation of value network type configuration 16
Figure 6 Value network of a hotel 17
Figure 7 Life cycle process area events 18
Figure 8 Business Process Event Management.. 19
Figure 9 Subprocess sales and reservation of an event (BPMN detail logic) 19
Figure 10: Platforms and tools for BPM 22
Figure 11 Automation of a process with a Process Engine, source: [1].................... 25
Figure 12 Scenario of a business in Industry 4.0 with IoT 33
Figure 13 Customized business process orchestration... 34
Figure 14 Baldrige Criteria for Performance Excellence Framework 58
Figure 15 Criteria for Performance Excellence 60
Figure 16 EFQM Model Structure (2013) 67
Figure 17 RADAR Cycle.. 70
Figure 18 The EFQM Model 2020 73
Figure 19: Singapore Business Excellence Framework... 75
Figure 20 Dubai Business Excellence Framework, 2020 77
Figure 21 Example of a BPM Governance implementation for Baldrige Model 81
Figure 22 forming a unit DevOps 83
Figure 23 DevOps framework – Based on work performed by Intel......................... 83
Figure 24 DevOPs integration concept to achieve greater business agility 85
Figure 25 TRADE methodology, Dr. Robin Mann 91
Figure 26 TRADE benchmarking process described using a process flow chart 92

Figure 27 BPIR's improvement cycle showing key services/information types available to support each activity in the cycle 94
Figure 28 TRADE Best Practice Certification System, 2018 96
Figure 29 Fishbone diagram of vehicle availability.. 98

7.4 About the Authors

Dr. Bernhard Hitpass is Associate Professor of the Universidad Técnica Federico Santa Maria (UTFSM), Executive Director BPM Center UTFSM, Director of the Postgraduate Certificate Program in BPM, Coaching and Business Consulting, Researcher in modeling and management techniques in the areas of Business Architectures, BPM and the BPMN standard. Masters coordinator and guest professor of other national and international universities.

He studied and hold a Master of Economics at Johannes Gutenberg Universität, Mainz, Germany, and a doctor degree at UNINI University in México. He is Author of the book, BPM Concepts, and How to Apply and Integrate it with IT, Author of the Spanish version of the international book BPMN 2.0 Reference Manual and Practical Guide. He is also the author and co-author of many current academic publications. Former CTO of the German IT Company Software AG in Chile, Former Director of Board the German multinational BI Company MIS AG in Brazil and Chile. In the 90s he was in Germany a researcher, consultant and teacher in the areas of Strategic Systems Planning and Requirement Engineering, he participated in international forums and in several publications. He has held different management positions in organizations and companies in Europe and Latin America. Within this scope he has taken charge of corporate projects related to the Business Process Management, Business Intelligence, Critical Missions Systems development and Organizational Development issues. He has a vast experience in the management of corporate projects.

Dr. Jorge J. Román Gárate is Excellence & Pioneering International Consultant for Dubai Police in UAE. He holds a PhD in Management from Lleida University in Spain, a Mechanical Engineer with a MBA from NSU, Tulsa-Oklahoma, USA. His areas of expertise focus on the application of Quality Improvement to business in service and products (Benchmarking for Best Practices, Lean Management, Business Excellence Framework). He is a part-time professor at University of Chile (Business and economic School), University of Piura in Peru, Guest Professor University Federico Santa María in Chile and Panamerican Business School in Guatemala.

Past-ASQ Chile Country Counselor 2014-2018, International Academy for Quality (Member), Organizational Excellence Technical Committee of the Quality Management Division, ASQ, Vice Chairman (2011-2013) of Global Benchmarking Network (GBN), Global Performance Excellence Award Executive Committee, International examiner for the Baldrige Training Program, Senior Examiner for the Iberoamerican Quality Award, and APQO (life time member). Subject Matter Expert for the Abu Dhabi Award for Excellence in Government Performance. Steering Committee Member – ASQ Organizational Excellence Technical Committee. Board of Judge at The International Best Practice Competition. International Journal of Excellence in Government, editorial board. Quality Management Forum (QMF) Editorial Review Board (A Peer-Reviewed Publication of the Quality Management Division of the American Society for Quality). Member of the Scientific Council at Dubai Police. Member of the International Advisor Board Policing Insight Magazine in UK. Global Presence: Speaker in business excellence and Benchmarking national and international levels. Author of the book Six Steps to Building a Culture of Quality.

8 REFERENCES

[1] J. Freund, B. Rücker y B. Hitpass, BPMN Manual de Referencia y Guía Práctica, BPM Center, Santiago de Chile, 5 ed., BHH, 2017.

[2] B. Hitpass, BPM Business Process Management, Fundamentos y Conceptos de Implementación, 4a Edición actualizada y ampliada ed., B. Center, Ed., Santiago: BHH Ltda, 2017.

[3] B. Hitpass y H. Astudillo, «Industry 4.0 challenges for business process management and electronic-commerce,» *Journal of theoretical and applied electronic commerce research,* vol. 14, n° 1, pp. I-III, 2019.

[4] B. Hitpass, Business Process Management - Introducción a gestión orientada a procesos, B. Center, Ed., Santiago de Chile: BHH Ltda, 2018.

[5] B. Hitpass, BPM - Concepts and How to Apply and Integrate it with IT, B. Center, Ed., Santiago: BHH Ltda., 2014.

[6] H. Smith y P. Fingar, Business Process Management (BPM): The Third Wave, Meghan-Kiffer Press, 2002.

[7] P. Harmon, «Process Governance,» *BP-Trends,* vol. 6, n° 3, 2008.

[8] J. Jeston y J. Nelis, Business Process Management- Practical Guidelines to Successful Implementations, Second Edition ed., 2008.

[9] M. Kirchmer, High Performance Through Process Excellence, From Strategy to Operations, Springer, 2009.

[10] C. Stabell y Ø. Fjeldstad, «Configuring Value for Competitive Advantage: On chains, Shops and Networks,» *Strategic Management Journal, Vol. 19,* pp. 413-437, 1998.

[11] H. Schmelzer, Geschäftsprozessmanagement in der Praxis, 6 ed., München: Hanser, 2008.

[12] T. Bellinson, «BPTrends Column,» *BP Trends,* 2016.

[13] F. Schönthaler, D. Augenstein y T. Karle, «Design and Governance of Collaborative Business Processes in Industry 4.0,» de *Proceedings of the Workshop on Crossorganizational and Cross-company BPM (XOC-BPM) co-located with the 17th IEEE Conference on Business Informatics (CBI 2015),*

Lisbon, 2015.

[14] J. Rifkin, The Zero Marginal Cost Society: The Internet of Things, the Collaborative Commons, and the Eclipse of Capitalism, Basingstoke, Hampshire, 2014.

[15] S. M. Ross, «Three imperatives for your digital transformation,» *MIT Sloan CISR,* vol. 16, n° 8, 2016.

[16] S. S. d. I. I. Chile, «Plan Estrategico 2019 - 2023,» SII, Santiago de Chile, 2019.

[17] J. A. Martinez, «Consorcio blockchain: el nuevo paso para el mercado financiero,» *EL Mercurio,* 09 Septiembre 2019.

[18] Government of Estonia, «e-estonia.com,» [En línea]. [Último acceso: 2020].

[19] J. Shen, «thomsonreuters.com,» Thomson Reuters, 20 12 2016. [En línea]. Available: https://blogs.thomsonreuters.com/answerson/e-estonia-power-potential-digital-identity/. [Último acceso: 2020].

[20] R. Geissbauer, J. Vedsø y S. Schrauf, «A Strategist's Guide to Industry 4.0,» *Strategy and Business,* vol. Summer 2016, n° 83, 2016.

[21] P. Tasatanattakool y C. Techapanupreeda, «Blockchain: Challenges and applications,» de *Proceedings of the International Conference on Information Networking (ICOIN),* Chiang Mai, 2018.

[22] V. B. Vukšić, M. P. Bach y A. Popovič, «Supporting performance management with business process management and business intelligence: A case analysis of integration and orchestration,» *International journal of information management,* vol. 4, n° 33, pp. 613-619, 2013.

[23] J. Garcia-Sabater y J. Marin-Garcia, «Enablers and inhibitors for sustainability of continuous improvement: A study in the automotive industry suppliers in the Valencia Region,» *Intagible Capital,* vol. 5, n° 2, pp. 183-209, 2009.

[24] A. Silva, C. Medeiros y R. Vieira, «Cleaner Production and PDCA cycle:Practical application for reducing the Cans Loss Index in a beverage company,» *Journal of Cleaner Production,* vol. 150, pp. 324-338, 2017.

[25] H. Darmawan, S. Hasibuan y H. Hardi-Purba, «Application of Kaizen Concept with 8 Steps PDCA to Reduce in Line Defect at Pasting Process: A Case Study in Automotive Battery,» *Journal of Optimization in Industrial Engineering,* vol. 4, pp. 97-107, 2018.

[26] S. Conger, Six Sigma and Business Process Management, vol. Handbook on Business Process Management 1, 2010, pp. 127-148.

[27] M. Imai, Gemba Kaizen, MacGraw-Hill, 1997.

[28] B. M. F. Suarez, El KAIZEN: La filosofía de mejora continua e innovación incremental detrás de la administración por calidad total, México: Panorama, 2007.

[29] J. K. Liker, The Toyota Way: 14 Management Principles from the World Greatest Manufacturer, New York: MCGraw-Hill, 2004.

[30] L. Cautrecasa, Lean Management: La gestión Competitiva por excelencia, Barcelona: Profit Editorial, 2010.

[31] J. Dahlgaard, J.-Y. J. Chi-Kuang Chen, L. Banegas y S. M. Dahlgaard-Park, «Business excellence models: limitations, reflections and further development,» *Journal Total Quality Management and Business Excellence,* vol. 24, nº 5, pp. 519-538, 2013.

[32] B. G. Dale, D. Bamford y A. van der Wiele, «An Essential Guide and Resource Gateway,» de *Managing Quality*, Chichester, 2016.

[33] P. Sampaio, P. Saraiva y A. Monteiro, «A comparison and usage overview of business excellence models,» *The TQM Journal,* vol. 24, nº 2, pp. 181-200, 2012.

[34] B. 20-20, «An Executive's Guide to the Criteria for Performance Excellence,» *National Institute of Standards and Technology,* 2011.

[35] B. 11-12, «Baldrige Performance Excellence Program - 2011–2012 Criteria for Performance Excellence,» *National Institute of Standards and Technology,*.

[36] M. Brown, Baldrige Award Winning Quality: How to Interpret the Baldrige Criteria for Performance Excellence, New York: Productivity Press: New York, 2008.

[37] National Institute of Standards and Technology (NIST), «www.nist.gov,» 2007. [En línea]. Available: http://www.nist.gov/public_affairs/baldrige_2005/sunnyfresh.htm. [Último acceso: 2020].

[38] EFQM, «Modelo EFQM de Excelencia,» EFQM Publications, 2013.

[39] European Foundation for Quality Management (EFQM), «www.efqm.org,» 2019. [En línea]. Available: http://www.efqm.org/what-we-

do/recognition/efqm-award-history. [Último acceso: 2020].

[40] R. Mann, «BPIR.com,» 30 10 2019. [En línea]. Available: BPIR.com. [Último acceso: 2020].

[41] T. Ahrens, «Tracing the evolution of the Dubai Government Excellence Program,» *Journal of Economic and Administrative Sciences,* vol. 30, n° 1, pp. 2-15, 2014.

[42] M. Zairi, «Shaping the future of government through excellence: How the UAE Government has taken lead International Journal of Excellence in Government,» *International Journal of Excellence in Government,* vol. 1, n° 1, pp. 2-7, 2019.

[43] IASA International Association of Software Architects, «DevOPs,» *Weekly Newsletter from Iasa Globa,* vol. 18, n° 5, 01 05 2020.

[44] R. Camp, Global cases in benchmarking: Best practices from organizations around the world, Milwaukee: ASQ Quality Press, 1998.

[45] M. Zairi y M. Al-Mashri, «The role of benchmarking in best practice management and knowledge sharing,» *The Journal of Computer Information Systems,* vol. 45, n° 4, p. 14, 2005.

[46] L. Mann, D. Samson y C. J. R. Wolfram, «Benchmarking as a mixed metaphor: Disentangling assumptions of competition and collaboration,» *Journal of Management Studies,* vol. 34, n° 2, pp. 285-314, 1997.

[47] B. Bartley, S. Gomibuchi y R. Mann, «Best practices in achieving a customer-focused culture,» *Benchmarking and International Journal,* vol. 14, n° 4, pp. 482-496, 2007.

[48] S. Codlings, Best Practice Benchmarking: An International Perspective, Indiana: Gulf Publishing Company, 1996.

[49] Germany Trade and Invest (GTAI), «Promoted by Federal Ministry for Economic Affairs and Energy in Accordance with a german Pairlaiment resolution,» Berlin, 2016.

[50] J. Rifkin, «The Zero Marginal Cost Society: The Internet of Things, the Collaborative Commons, and the Eclipse of Capitalism,» *Palgrave Macmillan,* 2014.

[51] G. Watson, Strategic Benchmarking: How to rate your company's performance against the World's Best, Toronto : Toronto Wiley Canada, 1993.

www.ingramcontent.com/pod-product-compliance
Lightning Source LLC
Chambersburg PA
CBHW071421210526
45465CB00001B/480